THE CHRISTIAN LIFE DELINEATED,

IN SEVERAL PRACTICAL DISCOURSES.

CHRIST TO BE FOUND IN THE ORDINANCES, WITH THE IMPORT AND HAPPY EFFECTS OF FINDING HIM.

Prov. viii. 35.—For whoso findeth me, findeth life, and shall obtain favour of the Lord. 489

SINNERS INTERESTED IN CHRIST, OBTAINING FAVOUR OF THE LORD.

Prov. viii. 35.—Whoso findeth me, shall obtain favour of the Lord. ... 521

UNBELIEF THE SIN AGAINST CHRIST BY WAY OF EMINENCE, AND THE WRONG DONE TO THE SOUL THEREBY.

Prov. viii. 36.—But he that sinneth against me, wrongeth his own soul; all they that hate me love death. 533

BELIEVERS A MYSTERY, WITH A DESCRIPTION OF THEIR TRAVELS FROM THE WILDERNESS OF THIS WORLD, TO THE HEAVENLY CANAAN, LEANING UPON CHRIST.

Song viii. 5.—Who is this that cometh up from the wilderness, leaning upon her beloved? 550

ENOCH'S CHARACTER AND TRANSLATION EXPLAINED, WITH A DESCRIPTION OF WALKING WITH GOD, AS THAT IN WHICH THE LIFE OF RELIGION LIES.

Gen. v. 24.—And Enoch walked with God, and he was not, for God took him. 580

THE
CHRISTIAN LIFE DELINEATED,
IN SEVERAL PRACTICAL DISCOURSES.

CHRIST TO BE FOUND IN THE ORDINANCES, WITH THE IMPORT AND HAPPY EFFECTS OF FINDING HIM.*

PROVERBS viii. 35,

For whoso findeth me, findeth life, and shall obtain favour of the Lord.

THIS chapter represents to us Wisdom speaking openly and most earnestly to her hearers. The discourse begins, ver. 4, and goes on to the end of the chapter.

It may here be enquired, 1. Who or what is this wisdom that speaks? I answer, Jesus Christ, the personal Wisdom of God; Luke xi. 49; 1 Cor. i. 24, in both which passages Christ is expressly called "the Wisdom of God." This appears from the personal properties ascribed to this Wisdom, as, (1.) Subsistence, ver. 30, "Then I was by him, as one brought up with him; and I was daily his delight." Compare John i. 1, "In the beginning was the Word, and the Word was with God, and the Word was God." (2.) The manner of subsistence, namely, eternal generation: vers. 22—24, "The Lord possessed me in the beginning of his way, before his works of old. I was set up from everlasting, from the beginning, or ever the earth was. When there was no depths, I was brought forth; when there was no fountains abounding with water." (3.) Personal attributes and effects; vers. 14—17, &c., "Counsel is mine, and sound wisdom; I am understanding, I have strength," &c.

It may be inquired, 2. To whom he speaks? I answer, "To men," ver. 4, "Unto you, O men, I call, and my voice is to the sons of men;" sinful and ruined men, who stand in need of salvation.

3. It may be inquired, What he speaks? I answer, The sum of it all is to commend itself to their souls, from their eternal happi-

---

* The substance of several sermons preached at Ettrick, in the year 1721.

ness, ver. 11, and downwards, "for wisdom is better than rubies; and all the things that may be desired, are not to be compared to it," &c.

4. What is the application of this discourse? It is an exhortation to hear his voice, comply with it, and close with him, ver. 32, and downwards, "Now therefore hearken unto me," &c.

In the two last verses is the conclusion of the whole matter.

(1.) Happiness is wrapt up in the enjoyment of him; ver. 35, "For whoso findeth me, findeth life, and shall obtain favour of the Lord."

(2.) Ruin is inevitable in the rejecting of him; ver. 36, "But he that sinneth against me, wrongeth his own soul; all they that hate me love death."

The former is the subject of our text; in which consider,

1. The connection with the preceding words, "For;" shewing them to be the reason of the blessedness pronounced on those that "hear him, watching daily at his gates," &c. These gates are the ordinances. It is supposed that he comes out at these gates, and so men being found watching at them, find him when he is pleased to come forth. It is a metaphor, which may be taken either, (1.) From scholars, whose hearts being set on learning, wait on at the schooldoor, till they can get in; or, (2.) From courtiers: Esth. ii. 21, or others waiting for access to their prince. (3.) Or from clients waiting on their advocates, or their judges late and early. Or, (4.) From lovers, who will hang on, watching for a meeting; Job xxxi. 9. They that thus watch and wait at Christ's gates, till he come forth, for getting their errand, are made up for ever. Which is the import of,

2. The words themselves; describing the happiness of those that find Christ. Wherein there are two things:—

1*st*, The happy man in heaven's account, "Whoso findeth me." It imports, that it is not every one that comes to his gates that finds him; many go as they came; but some do find him. The world counts him the happy man that finds riches, honours, pleasures, &c., like Ephraim, who said, "I am become rich, I have found me out substance;" Hos. xii. 8; and therefore they watch and wait greedily where they may have them, saying, "Who will shew us any good?" Psalm iv. 6. But when they have found what they were seeking, it often appears, that they have been seeking and have found their own ruin. But he is happy indeed that finds Christ, for he finds an upmaking treasure.

2*dly*, The happiness of that man; which lies in two things,

(1.) He that finds Christ "finds life." Without him we are dead men; but falling on Christ the fountain of life, as the man's dead body on the bones of Elisha; 2 Kings xiii. 21, the soul gets life, eternal life, that will never die out any more. [*Heb.* hath found;] in finding me, he hath found life; 1 John v. 12, "He that hath the Son, hath life."

(2.) He " shall obtain favour of the Lord ;" for the Father is well pleased with Christ, and with all who are in him. He shall be accepted with the Lord; Eph. i. 6. The sky shall clear on him, which was lowring before. Heaven shall smile on him. Yea, he shall bring forth favour from the Lord, as out of a treasure now opened to him; so the word intimates.

From the connection of the text with the preceding context, we may observe the two following doctrines, viz:—

DOCTRINE I. The ordinances are the place where Christ is to be found of poor sinners.

DOCT. II. People may come to ordinances, and yet not find Christ.

I shall discuss these two doctrines before I enter on the words themselves.

DOCT. I. The ordinances are the place where Christ is to be found of poor sinners.

In handling this doctrine, I shall,

I. Shew what are the ordinances in which Christ is to be found.

II. Confirm the doctrine.

III. *Lastly*, Apply.

I. I am to shew what are the ordinances wherein, especially, Christ is to be found. If any of you have Job's desire; Job xxiii. 3, " O that I knew where I might find him!" I would direct you to " go out by the footsteps of the flock ;" Cant. i. 8, where to find him. These ordinances are,

1. The divine ordinance of meditation; Hag. i. 5, " Thus saith the Lord of hosts, consider your ways." Here is the first sight ofttimes that a sinner gets of Christ; as did the prodigal son; Luke xv. 17, " When he came to himself, he said, How many hired servants of my father's have bread enough and to spare, and I perish with hunger!" Therefore David adviseth his enemies to this; Psalm iv. 4, " Commune with your own heart upon your bed." And here the saints have often got renewed sights of him, to their soul's satisfaction; Psalm lxiii. 5, 6, " My soul shall be satisfied as with marrow and fatness; and my mouth shall praise thee with joyful lips; when I remember thee upon my bed, and meditate on thee in the night watches." What is it that keeps Christ and many sinners

asunder, but that really they will not come near this gate of wisdom? They will not think on their case.

2. Christian conference about spiritual matters. Hence we read of this being practised in a very declining time; Mal. iii. 16, "Then they that feared the Lord, spake often one to another. This was the gate at which the two disciples found and met with Christ; Luke xxiv. 32, "Did not our hearts burn within us," say they, "while he talked with us by the way, and while he opened to us the scriptures?" As two cold flint stones struck one upon another produce fire; so doth spiritual conference sometimes warm cold hearts; Cant. v. 8, 9, and vi. 1. Meetings for Christian fellowship have been meeting-places with Christ to many; the due consideration whereof might well encourage and stir up Christians to a more frequent attendance upon them.

3. Singing of the Lord's praises. This is a commanded duty; Eph. v. 18, 19—"Be filled with the Spirit; speaking to yourselves in psalms, and hymns, and spiritual songs, singing and making melody in your heart to the Lord." What made David so frequently to wait on about this gate, but that he knew the King used to come forth that way? Here Paul and Silas got a joyful meeting with Christ even in a prison; Acts xvi. 25, 26. It is pity, that people should treat it as a blind gate, at which they never look for the Lord to come forth. But in the experience of the Lord's people he is to be found there. The heavenly melody sometimes melts hard hearts, elevates drooping souls, and fills them with glowing affection to Christ.

4. Prayer. It is called seeking of God, and is the highway to find him. It has a large promise; Matth. vii. 7, "Ask, and it shall be given you; seek, and ye shall find; knock, and it shall be opened unto you;" and it has been the gate of heaven to many a soul. It is a four-leaved gate, and at every one of the leaves the King has shewn himself to poor sinners. (1.) Public prayer, at which Lydia got her heart opened; Acts xvi. 13, 14. (2.) Private prayer, whether in one's family; Acts x. 30, or otherwise in society with others privately; Acts xii. 12. This social prayer has a large promise made to it; Matth. xviii. 19, "I say unto you, That if two of you shall agree on earth, as touching any thing that they shall ask, it shall be done for them of my Father which is in heaven." (3.) Secret prayer. Many a soul has found Christ there. There Jacob got the blessing; Gen. xxxii. 24. There Daniel beheld the King in his glory, and obtained favour; Dan. ix. 22. This has many a time made the corner of a barn, byre, or dyke-side, a Bethel, a Peniel; and these are more esteemed than a king's palace, by the children of God. (4.)

Ejaculatory prayer. This has many times suddenly opened, to the soul's finding of Christ. So it did with Moses; Exod. xiv. 15, "Wherefore criest thou unto me? speak unto the children of Israel, that they go forward;" and with Nehemiah, chap. ii. 4. No wonder they do not find him, that watch not at this gate.

5. The word. This is the most patent door of heaven, at which the King usually comes forth to his attendants, that come to wait on him there. It is a two-leaved gate. (1.) The word read, Rev. i. 3, "Blessed is he that readeth." Augustine hearing a voice, Take up and read, opened Rom. xiii. 12, 13, and was converted. Junius was brought to Christ by reading John i. (2.) The word preached, 1 Cor. i. 21,—"It pleased God by the foolishness of preaching to save them that believe. This is a well of salvation at which three thousand persons at a time drank and lived, Acts ii. 41. The eunuch met with Christ at this gate, where the one, viz. hearing the word, opened after the other, viz. reading the word; and he found favour with the Lord.

6. *Lastly*, The sacraments, baptism and the Lord's supper. These are sealing ordinances, in which many have had sensible communion with Jesus Christ. It is true, the first finding of him is not to be expected here; but though they are not converting, they are confirming ordinances; and as such, happy means of strengthening the believer's faith and love, and increasing his acquaintance with Christ.

II. In order to confirm this doctrine, consider,

1. The ordinances are by Christ's own appointment the trysting-places, wherein he has promised to be found of those that seek him; Exod. xx. 24, "In all places where I record my name, I will come unto thee, and I will bless thee." So that coming thither to wait on him, they may expect to find him there. It is the divine appointment put upon them, which is accompanied with a blessing, that gives ground of hope in the case. By this they are,

(1.) Trysting places for sinners; where they may be convinced, converted, and regenerated; James i. 18, "Of his own will begat he us with the word of truth." These are the pools where the Spirit troubles the water for the cure of sinners of their deadly soul diseases. And there Christ and the sinner meet, for making up the spiritual match. (2.) Trysting places for saints; where they may receive life more abundantly, 1 Pet. ii. 2, 3. In them he keeps his lower table for the feeding of those to whom he has given life. They are the inns in the way to Immanuel's land; the pools in the way to Zion, the wells of salvation.

2. They are the places wherein his people seek him, who know best where he is to be found. When the spouse had lost sight of her

beloved, she goes to the ordinances to seek him; Cant. iii. 2, " I will rise now," says she, " and go about the city in the streets, and in the broad ways I will seek him whom my soul loveth." And they are the places where his people have found him, and do find him; Cant. vii. 5, " The king is held in the galleries." So it is even as natural to them to go to these duties and ordinances when they would see him, as for a child to seek out the mother, in the place where she is wont to be. And when they find him not in one duty, they go to another, till going the little further they find him.

3. They are what the Lord has allowed his people to supply the want of heaven, until they come there; the tabernacle set up in the wilderness, till they get the temple in Canaan. And therefore they must last till then and no longer; Eph. iv. 11, 12, 13, " And he gave some, apostles; and some prophets; and some evangelists: and some, pastors and teachers; for the perfecting of the saints, for the work of the ministry, for the edifying of the body of Christ; till we all come in the unity of the faith, and of the knowledge of the Son of God, unto a perfect man, unto the measure of the stature of the fulness of Christ." When John saw the new Jerusalem, he made that observe on it; Rev. xxi. 22, " I saw no temple therein; for the Lord God Almighty, and the Lamb, are the temple of it." But they could not supply that place, unless Christ were there; but he is there; Matth. xxviii. ult., " Lo, I am with you alway, even unto the end of the world." Cant. iv. 6, " Until the day break, and the shadows flee away, I will get me to the mountain of myrrh, and to the hill of frankincense."

III. *Lastly*, I come now to apply this doctrine.

USE I. Of reproof. It reproves,

1. Those who slight attendance on ordinances, public, private, or secret. It is much to be lamented that there are so many who do so, and that so little prevails with many to do it. Ah! sirs, if ye look on this practice in its true colours, it is a slighting of Christ, and an opportunity of meeting with him. It is a breaking of the appointment which the Son of God has made with you; and if the appointment be broken must not the business you have with him stick?

2. Those who will come to ordinances to meet with some that they have worldly business with. They will come to the church on the Lord's day, because they have somebody to meet there, perhaps a servant to bespeak, &c. This is a grossly profane abuse of the ordinances of the Lord; a turning of that which Christ appointed for the service of your souls, to the service of your lusts; a turning of that which is appointed for your eternal interest into your carnal interests. What will these say, when Christ rises up to plead with them at the

great day? when they shall hear, that his being to be found there, could not bring them there; but they would go for fellow-worms, to transact business with them?

3. Those who come to ordinances, but seek not to find Christ there; of such the Lord speaks; Isa. xxix. 13, "This people draw near me with their mouth, and with their lips do they honour me, but have removed their heart far from me." How many go to prayers, sermons, &c., who have it not in their view to meet with Christ in them? So they come away without him, and they do not mourn because they find him not; and how can they be so affected, since it was not their errand to meet with him?

4. Those who stand in the way of others attending on ordinances. The effect of this is to keep them out of Christ's way, and to hinder their keeping appointment with the Son of God; by which they become answerable for all the damage that thereupon ensues to the souls of such; Luke xi. 52, "Wo unto you, lawyers! for ye have taken away the key of knowledge; ye entered not in yourselves, and them that were entering in, ye hindered.."

Use II. Seek Christ in ordinances, and come to them with a design to find Christ there. When ye go to read the word, to secret duties, or family duties, or public ordinances, think with yourselves, "I am going to wisdom's gates, O shall I not see the King's face? find the smell of his garments, get some communion with Christ?" When Mary missed him in his grave, she could not be satisfied with a vision of angels, but wept on, till she found him, John xx. 11—16. O that there were such a heart in us! For motives to enforce this exhortation, consider,

1. He is well worth the seeking. "He that findeth Christ, findeth life." If his transcendent beauty and peerless excellencies were known, we could not but seek him till we had found him; John iv. 10, "If thou knewest the gift of God," says Christ to the woman of Samaria, "and who it is that saith to thee, Give me to drink; thou wouldst have asked of him, and he would have given thee living water." They that find him are made up for time and eternity. When ye come to ordinances, know ye where ye are? Ye are upon a beautiful field, and it may be your own. Ye see the surface of it, but know ye what is in the bowels of it? A treasure, and Christ is that treasure, Matth. xiii. 44. The ordinances are the earthen vessels, but there is a treasure in them, 2 Cor. iv. 7.

2. That is what the people of God have been seeking, and are intent upon in ordinances, in all ages, however careless the blind world has been about it. And they sought always again, because they had once found; they still desired to drink of that fountain,

after they had once tasted of it. Hence says David; Psalm xxvii. 4, "One thing have I desired of the Lord, that will I seek after, that I may dwell in the house of the Lord, all the days of my life, to behold the beauty of the Lord, and to inquire in his temple. Psalm lxiii. 2, "My flesh longeth for thee, to see thy power and thy glory, so as I have seen thee in the sanctuary. When Jacob found himself engaged with Christ, how intent was he? Gen. xxxii. 24, "I will not let thee go, except thou bless me." This has made them follow ordinances to the fields and the mountains, at the hazard of their lives by persecutors; and they thought all hardships little enough, to find Christ in them.

3. What avail ordinances, if ye do not find Christ in them? Upon this consideration, we should take Moses' protestation before we go to them; Exod. xxxiii. 15, "If thy presence go not with me, carry us not up hence." They are but empty husks without him, and cannot feed the soul; he is the marrow and sap of them; John vi. 63, "The words that I speak unto you, they are spirit, and they are life." Mary met with a disappointment, when she saw two angels in the sepulchre, but Christ himself was away. Should the man that has a petition for life, be brought before the chair of state, but his prince not in; would he not say, "Alas! it is the king alone himself that can do my business;" so here, when the soul seeks Christ, ordinances alone will not satisfy it; no, the man wants to enjoy Christ in them, as he alone is suited to his case.

4. *Lastly*, It is a great pity ye should not meet, when the parties have come so far on the appointment. And,

(1.) Most of you come hither from a considerable distance; it is pity you should forget your errand when ye are come. Ye come too far for nothing; the pains and toil of waiting on ordinances, I think, should even stir you up to think with yourselves, "What am I at this pains for? what am I seeking? shall I make nothing for my soul by it?"

(2.) But Christ came farther for it than any of you to keep this appointment, and it cost him infinitely dearer than it does any of you. It cost him a long journey from heaven to earth; to sweat drops of blood, and to lose his precious life on a cross, ere there could be a possibility of your meeting with him in ordinances. And now when he is come, shall the meeting misgive betwixt him and your souls? But I must proceed to consider,

DOCT. II. People may come to ordinances, and yet not find Christ. One may be found at Christ's palace gates, and yet never see the King come forth; as Absalom did in another case.

Here I shall give the reasons why it is so, and then apply the point.

I. I am to offer some reasons why sinners may come to ordinances, and not find Christ. And these are all on the sinner's side.

1. Some have no design of finding Christ in ordinances at all; they have no such thing as a meeting with Christ before their eyes. But the Sabbath-day is an idle day, and they will go to the church, and see and be seen, Isa. i. 12. May be they like to hear the preaching, as they would like a lovely song to divert them. But for a Christ in the preaching, a Saviour for their lost souls, manifested therein; that is what never comes in their head. They are like Ezekiel's hearers, of whom the Lord says, chap. xxxiii. 31, 32, "They come unto thee as the peeple cometh, and they sit before thee as my people, and they hear thy words, but they will not do them: for with their mouth they shew much love, but their heart goeth after covetousness. And lo, thou art unto them as a very lovely song of one that hath a pleasant voice, and can play very well on an instrument: for they hear thy words, but they do them not.

2. Many are indifferent whether they find Christ in ordinances or not. And by their indifferency they even court a denial from the King. They are not at pains to tryst with him, in earnest, before they come to public ordinances. They do not prepare for the meeting, by casting down the idols of jealousy, 1 Pet. ii. 1, 2. Their spirits are very flat, and their desires languid when at ordinances; they are not fervent in spirit, serving the Lord. They stand at the palace-gate, but they do not ask, seek, and knock, Matth. vii. 7, and go their way contented, though they do not find him.

3. Some desire not to see him at all; Job xxi. 14, "They say unto God, Depart from us; for we desire not the knowledge of thy ways; they are well content he shew not himself to them. If his harbingers which go before him, namely, convictions of guilt and danger, once begin to appear, they quickly shut their eyes, and will be very desirous to get out of their way. They have no heart for the match with the Lord of glory, and so care not for coming to a treaty about it.

4. *Lastly*, Some who may have desires of meeting with Christ, yet cannot away with on-waiting at the gates, and going about from one gate to another, till they find him. We are naturally addicted to unbelieving haste, John vii. 6. If the Lord do not keep our time which we set, we conclude he will never come, Psalm cxvi. 11. But faith is a waiting grace, and sets no time, but persists in that exercise, Isa. xxviii. 16, Lam. iii. 49, 50. Now the King, to try of what metal people's desires after him are, delays long his coming forth; and by the time that he comes, as it were, the throng is away from about the palace-gate, and there remains only here and there

one whom the grace of God has endued with a principle of on-waiting. And O how heavy is it to think, that some who have gone far to find Christ, have lost him for not going a little farther! Some have waited long, and have lost him for not waiting but a little longer. The Israelites waited for Moses till the thirty-ninth day; had they but waited the fortieth day, they would not have made and worshipped the golden calf, Exod. xxxii. 5. Saul waited for Samuel till the seventh day; had he waited a few hours longer, he had not offered sacrifices unwarrantably, and been stript of his kingdom, 1 Sam. xiii. 8, &c.

I shall now make some short improvement of this point.

Seek Christ so in ordinances, as ye may find him. That is,

1. Seek him sincerely and uprightly with all your heart, Deut. iv. 29. They are blessed that so seek him, Psalm cxix. 2. Seeking from the teeth outward, may prevail with those who know not men's hearts; but not with him, who knows the language of the heart, without an interpreter. It is true, in a way of sovereignty, he may be found of those that seek him not, Isa. lxv. 1, and love may make a net for a false heart; but who can promise on that?

2. Seek him honestly and generously for himself, Psalm cv. 4. Ye hear of his glorious matchless excellencies, let your hearts be caught in the net of his love. And let not his benefits be your only or main inducement, like those mentioned, John vi. 26, of whom our Lord says, "Ye seek me, not because ye saw the miracles, but because ye did eat of the loaves, and were filled;" for that casts contempt on his person. Sovereignty sometimes comes over this indeed, as in the case of Zaccheus.

3. Seek him fervently, Rom. xii. 11. How fervent was the Psalmist's heart, Psalm xlii. 1, "As the heart panteth after the waterbrooks, so panteth my soul after thee, O God." Psalm lxiii. 1, 2, "O God, thou art my God, early will I seek thee: my soul thirsteth for thee, my flesh longeth for thee in a dry and thirsty land, where no water is; to see thy power and thy glory, so as I have seen thee in the sanctuary." Drowsy desires and lazy wishes will not find him out, Cant. iii. 1, 2. Be warm and importunate in your addresses, and the King will come forth at length, Luke xviii. 7.

4. Seek him humbly, Psalm x. 17. The woman of Canaan is a noble instance of a humble seeker, Matth. xv. 23, &c. Beggars must not be choosers. Humility teaches to be thankful for a crumb, for a passing view of the King.

5. Seek him diligently, Heb. xi. 6. Careless seekers can hardly look to be finders. Seek diligently, as the spouse on considering her case did, leaving no corner of the city untouched, that she might

find him, Cant. iii. 2; as those who are searching for hidden treasure Prov. ii. 4, 5.

6. Seek him mournfully, Luke ii. 48. Mary did so, and found him, John xx. 11, &c., and Jacob also, Hos. xii. 4. When he withdraws, were one mourning for the want, it would be a hopeful sign. Lament after the Lord; there is good reason for it at this day.

7. *Lastly*, Seek him constantly, till ye find him, therein intimating the example of the church; Lam. iii. 49, 50, "Mine eye trickleth down and ceaseth not, without any intermission : till the Lord look down, and behold from heaven." Be resolute not to give over till ye have met with him, and be sure ye will not be disappointed in the end.

I come now to the words themselves. The happy man is he that findeth Christ. Finding of Christ is the upmaking of the soul, it is man's happiness; no wonder it be a big thing, comprehending much. I take it up in these two. (1.) A saving discovery of Christ made to the soul; so the word is used, Matth. xiii. 46, in the case of finding the pearl. (2.) An interest in him, yea, actual possession of him, as one's own obtained. So in our text, findeth life, *i. e.* really gets life. So they find him, who get such a discovery of him, as terminates in their closing with him, whereby he is theirs, and they are his.

The following doctrines offer themselves from the words now and formerly explained.

Doct. I. Then do people find Christ, when, upon a saving discovery of Christ made to their souls, they close with him by faith.

Doct. II. Sinners finding Christ, find life.

I shall handle each doctrine in order.

Doct. I. Then do people find Christ, when, upon a saving discovery of Christ made to their souls, they close with him by faith. This I shall explain and apply.

In explaining the doctrine, I shall,

I. Offer some things in the general touching the finding of Christ.

II. More particularly explain the soul's finding of Christ.

I. I am to offer some things in the general touching the finding of Christ. And,

1. There is a twofold finding of him; initial, and progressive.

1*st*, There is an initial finding of Christ, which is the soul's first finding of him, the first meeting betwixt Christ and the soul, Matth. xiii. 45, 46, when the dead soul meets with the life-giving Saviour. Upon this our salvation depends.

2*dly*, There is a progressive finding of him, which is a child of

God's finding of him in the progress of his state of grace, Matth. vii. 7. Thus the spouse found him, Cant. iii. 4, after some partial withdrawing from her.

The difference betwixt these two lies in this, that the immediate effect of the former is union, of the other, actual communion with Christ. The one is the marriage with Christ, the other the return of the husband to his deserted spouse. The text, I think, comprehends both; but the first mainly; compare ver. ult. And both consist of a discovery of Christ, and a receiving him; the latter as well as the former; the one initial, the other progressive. It is the first of these I intend.

2. There are some things to be observed touching this finding of Christ.

1*st*, Sinners in their natural state have lost God, Eph. ii. 12. God is not their God, they have no saving interest in him. There was a covenant of friendship betwixt God and innocent man; but, alas! that covenant was broken, and man quite lost his friend, his God. So he goes up and down the world, in his natural state, a poor friendless creature.

2*dly*, Man is a seeking creature;' for he cannot miss to know that he wants, nor to desire to have his wants supplied; Matth. xiii. 45. He goes through the creation, seeking something to satisfy his heart. And when one will not do, he goes to another. The soul of man, though in its blindness it knows not what it would be at, is still seeking; like a nest of young birds still gaping for meat from the dam.

3*dly*, There is no rest for, nor satisfying of the soul till it come to God. This is not from any desire the soul has of God while in its natural state, but ariseth from the natural state of it, whereby it comes to pass, that nothing less than an infinite good can satisfy it. Therefore the natural man is represented as one ever labouring, but never able to get rest; Matth. xi. 28, Isa. lv. 1, 2. And its life is a wandering and seeking without intermission; Matth. xiii. 45, 46.

4*thly*, God is in Christ, to be found in him, and in him only; 2 Cor. v. 19, Col. ii. 9. As the Israelites, who wandered forty years in the wilderness, had a tabernacle set up among them, where they might find God, which was called (Heb.) the tabernacle of meeting; so Jesus Christ is the true tabernacle of meeeting betwixt God and sinners; and he is no where else to be found. So that till the soul fall on Christ in its weary search, it can never come to God, nor to true rest.

II. I shall more particularly explain the soul's finding of Christ. There are two things in it.

First, The soul savingly discovers and discerns Jesus Christ, by a new light let into it; John xvii. 3. There is a twofold discovery of Christ. (1.) An objective discovery of him in the gospel, given to all who hear it. Thus the sun's light discovers all things in the presence of the blind man, but alas! he cannot perceive them for all that. (2) A subjective discovery, when the eyes of the understanding are opened to see what is so discovered; Acts xxvi. 18, Isa. xxxiii. 17. This is the finding of Christ, in respect of which the sinner is like Hagar near the well; Gen. xxi. 19. Jesus Christ is near the man; Rom. x. 8, but he sees him not, so still he wants him, till, the Lord opening his eyes, he discerns Christ, and so finds him. The soul then beholds him in a twofold glory.

1. The glory of his person, as God-man: an admirable person, a nonsuch, the chief among ten thousand, Cant. v. 10. The soul finding Christ, beholds him as the Father's fellow, the brightness of his glory, and the express image of his person; Heb i. 3, in respect of his divine nature; and as our kinsman, and the glory of mankind, in respect of his human nature; the flower of Adam's posterity, holy, harmless, undefiled, and separate from sinners.

2. The glory of his mediatory office, 1 Tim. ii. 5. The soul gets a sight of him, as the great Daysman betwixt God and sinners, fit to lay his hand on both parties. It beholds him as the tabernacle of meeeing, where God meets with the sinner to make up the peace; as that noble Personage appointed of the Father the repairer of the breach made by sin; the great Surety and Cautioner for sinners' debt and God's glory. And there are six things the soul now sees in Christ.

(1) A transcendent excellency, beauty, and loveliness in him; Isa. xxxiii. 17, Cant. v. *ult.* It sees him lovely in his natures, in his offices, in his holy life, and in his bloody death; lovely in himself, and in his purchase. It is a too common question that the daughters of Jerusalem put to the spouse; Cant. v. 9. What is thy beloved more than another beloved? The world sees no beauty in him, for which he is to be desired; they see more beauty in carnal worldly objects, than in the Plant of Renown. But no sooner does the soul find him, but it sees him lovely above all persons and things. His discovered excellency darkens all created glory, as the sun arising darkens the candle-light, and makes the stars hide their heads; Matth. xiii. 45, 46.

(2.) A fulness in him for the supply of all its wants; Col. i. 19, "It pleased the Father, that in him should all fulness dwell. There is, (1.) A fulness of the Godhead in him, Col. ii. 9. The soul that has lost God, finding him, finds God in him, John xiv. 11. (2.) A fulness of merit, for our justification, and a title to heaven. (3.) A fulness of Spirit, for our sanctification, and making us meet for heaven. Finding Christ, the soul finds a treasure, for preciousness, abundance, and variety.

(3.) A suitableness in him; and that is twofold.

[1.] A suitableness in Christ to their own case, as when a hungry man finds meat, or a naked man clothes, Rev. iii. 18. The soul of man goes through the creation, seeking a match in whom it may rest; but it never finds a suitable one till it find Christ. Still the bed is shorter than that it can stretch itself upon it, and the cover narrower than that it can wrap itself in it; but coming to Christ, the soul finds him completely suited to its case; suited to still and quiet the conscience by his atoning blood, and to satisfy its craving desires by his all-fulness. There appears, then, a suitableness in everything in and about him; in his natures, in his offices, in his life and death, resurrection, ascension, &c.

[2.] A suitableness in him to the glory of God. The sinner whose eyes are opened can never expect salvation but in a way suitable to God's perfections, his holiness and justice; and the mystery of Christ appears thus suited, 2 Cor. iv. 6. Here at once appears how justice is satisfied, and the sinner saved; and God has his glory and the sinner his salvation together.

(4.) The wisdom of God in him, 1 Cor. i. 24. The wisdom of God eminently appeared in the creation, and appears every day in the works of providence; but the master-piece of divine wisdom is the mystery of Christ, wherein is the greatest display of the divine perfections, his power, justice, holiness, mercy, love, goodness, and truth, all woven together by infinite wisdom. And there is none that finds Christ, but must say that that device is one becoming infinite wisdom.

(5.) An ability to save, Heb. vii. 25. When sin appears in its native colours to the awakened conscience, the soul is apt to question, if there be any balm in Gilead for such wounds; if there be any hope of such a case. But when Christ is discovered to the soul, he appears as the Lord of hosts, mighty to save; there is merit enough in his blood to wash away the deepest guilt, and efficacy enough in his Spirit to subdue the strongest corruptions.

(6.) *Lastly,* Willingness to save, and to communicate of his fulness to the needy soul, Heb. iv. 15, 16. The discovery of this was what brought the prodigal son home, Luke xv. 17, and the utter want of it must make the starving soul die in despondency. This is that which of all things awakened sinners have most ado to discern in Christ, if he be willing to save them, to bestow his precious blood to wash such vile wretches as they. But it is discovered in lesser or greater measure to all that find Christ.

Secondly, Upon this discovery of Christ made unto and by the soul, the soul closes with Christ by faith. There is such a connection betwixt these two, that (1.) None can close with Christ without it, Cant. v. 9. People may love an unseen Christ, but not an unknown Christ. (2.) All that get it close with him, Psalm ix. 10, John iv. 10. For,

1. Such a discovery of Christ is not made to the soul till it be hunger-bitten, lost in its own eyes, and would be content with a Saviour on any terms, Acts ix. 6, Prov. xxiv. 7. A starving person needs no other invitation to eat but to see meat; and when Christ is discovered to the soul lost in its own eyes, it will embrace him.

2. The nature of the object speaks for itself, John iv. 10. Christ discovered to the soul is precious, 1 Pet. ii. 7, and he who once finds the pearl, will gripe at it to make it his own. He is suitable to its case, which likewise insures the soul's closing with him, as the sick man with the physician, or the captive with the deliverer.

3. It is always attended with a heart-conquering power, Psalm cx. 3. When the Lord opens the eyes in saving illumination, he looses the heart by renewing the will, and so brings the soul to embrace Christ.

I shall now apply this branch of the subject.

Use I. Of information. This shews us,

1. They have never found Christ, nor seen his glory, who have not closed with him, Psalm ix. 10. They who have not matched with Christ, have never yet seen nor known the glorious Bridegroom, John i. 10, 11. For all they have heard of him in the word, or seen of him in the sacraments, they are still unacquainted with him, and he has ever been a vailed beauty to them. A look of him with an illuminated eye of the mind, would have conquered their souls to his love, Isa. xlv. 22.

2. They who reject Christ and his way, and think they have reason for so doing, must know that their judgment is not to be regarded; for they are blind men judging of colours. (1.) There are some who never made so much as a shew of trial of Christ and his way. They were estranged from God from the womb, and they held even forward in their course of sin to this day, without changing; and they are making lies of Christ to themselves and others, Psalm lviii. 3. Poor souls, they know no better, they are under soul-ruining delusion. If their eyes were opened, they would hate what they now love, and love what they now hate, Tit. iii. 3. (2.) There are others, who, after a seeming trial made of Christ and his

way, have cast them behind their back, 2 Pet. ii. 22. But neither have they ever got a discovery of him, for as long as they have hung on about Wisdom's gates, 1 Cor. ii. 8. They have got into the outer court, of prayer, the communion-table, a fair blooming profession; but they never got into the inner court, to see the King in his beauty. Let both know, that there is something in religion which they never knew to this day; and while they despise it, they despise what they know not. And if they knew what they know not, they would as soon embrace death and hell, and throw away their own life, as do what they do.

3. Ye who have got such a discovery of Christ as has determined you to close with him, ye have found Christ, and happy are ye. All the people of God have not alike sensible enjoyment of Christ, Matth. xvii. 1, 2, nor alike measure of manifestations of him. Neither are their comforts of alike height, more than their downcastings are of alike depth. But that discovery of Christ which terminates in the soul's closing with him, is saving.

Use II. Of trial. Hereby ye may try whether ever ye have found Christ or not. We have been long making the fashion of seeking, let us try whether we have come speed or not. If ye have got such a discovery of him, as has terminated in your souls' closing with him, ye have found him. And ye may know it by these marks,

Mark 1. If ye have found Christ, ye will value the discovery as a matchless favour, and display of free grace, Matth. xiii. 44. Like as a poor man, travelling through a desert, in want of all things, would value his finding a covered table and all necessaries; so will the soul that has been seeking rest through the empty creation, and is still disappointed, value the discovery of a full Christ made to it, Psalm cxix. 162. Ye will admire free grace in it, and not impute it to your own pains and diligence, that ever ye had any acquaintance with him.

Mark 2. A found Christ will engage your esteem above all other persons and things, 1 Pet. ii. 7. He will be in your eyes the chief among ten thousand. The world, and all that is in it will be but loss and dung in comparison of him, Psalm lxxiii. 25. However low thoughts ye had of him before, the market will be raised now, and the rate ye will put on him will be so high, as the compass of the whole world, nay, the compass of men's desires will not be able to afford an equivalent, and as good, Prov. viii. 11.

Mark 3. The discovery of Christ in his glory, will shew sin in ugly colours, and fill a soul with self-loathing and abhorrence, Job xlii. 5, 6; Isa. vi. 5. Delusion puffeth up, but real manifestations of Christ are humbling. As in the balances, one scale goes up when the other goes down; so the more Christ is exalted in the eyes of a sinner, the more sin and self are depressed. Doves' dung and asses' heads gave a great price in Samaria, when bread was not to be had, but when it came they were no more valued. That light will discover the worthlessness even of one's duties, and shew one's own righteousness like a moth-eaten garment, held up before the sun, Isa. lxiv. 6; and leave one poor in spirit before the Lord.

MARK 4. A found Christ will engage the sinner's heart and affections, loosing the bond betwixt them and other lovers, and dispose the soul to say, as Isa. xxvi. 13, "O Lord our God, other lords besides thee have had dominion over us; but by thee only will we make mention of thy name." There is an overcoming glory in him, which being discerned does infallibly give him the preference in the heart to all competitors, Tit. ii. 11. A believing view of his glory fills the heart with desire after him, and love to him above and beyond all other things, Isa. xxvi. 9; Cant. i. 3. Many a stroke the law, perhaps, has given to break the bonds of iniquity; but still they hold the sinner fast. But when the gospel fire is set on in the soul, and thereby Christ is discovered in his matchless excellency to the soul, these bonds are burnt and melted down.

MARK 5. Christ being found, the sinner parts with all for him, without reserve; and when he has quitted all for him, he thinks he has a good bargain, Matth. xiii. 46. Where any reserve is made, there is no saving discovery of Christ made there, who in his first appearance in the soul saith effectually, "If ye take me, let these go their way." The soul parts with all sin; (1.) In respect of affliction, Rom. vii. 19. (2) Of voluntary subjection, Rom. vi. 14. (3.) Of allowed residence, Rom. vii. 24. It parts with self too. (1.) Civil self, friends, credit, ease, &c., Luke xvi. 26; Heb. xi. 24, 25; Deut xxxiii. 9. (2.) Natural self, even life itself is at his disposal. All that a man hath will he give for his life; but one will not give a found Christ for it, Luke xiv. 26. And (3.) Religious self is parted with, whereby the soul "counts all things but loss, for the excellency of the knowledge of Christ," Phil. iii.

MARK 6. A saving discovery of Christ transforms the soul into his image. The sight of the most beautiful object on earth cannot work a likeness to it on the beholders; but a manifestation of Christ does it, 2 Cor. iii. 18. Love breeds likeness, and likeness nourishes love, and none see Christ in his glory, but they love him, and therefore do put on Christ, Rom xiii. ult.; labouring to walk as he walked, 1 John ii. 6. From that moment the soul finds Christ, it commences nonconformist to the world, being transformed, cast into another mould, in respect of nature and actions, Rom. xii. 2. And when at death the discovery shall be perfect, so will holiness be, 1 John iii. 2.

MARK 7. They that have once had a saving discovery of Christ, will always desire further discoveries of him, till they see him as he is, Exod. xxxiii. 18, "Shew me thy glory," will be the language of their hearts. Here we have the bridegroom's picture as it were in ordinances, in the word; and they who have once seen the beauty of it, will always be desiring more. Paul knew much of Christ, but his eye was not satisfied with seeing, Phil. iii. 10. Christ was the sum of his life, Phil. i. 21; the body of divinity to which he desired to confine his studies, 1 Cor. ii. 2; for in the knowledge of Christ all religion lies; therefore the learning of Christianity is the learning of Christ, Eph. iv. 20, 21.

DOCTRINE II. Sinners finding Christ, find life.

In discoursing from this doctrine, I shall;

I. Unfold that life which sinners find, finding Christ.

II. Confirm the point,

III. Make some practical improvement.

I. I shall unfold that life which sinners find finding Christ. They find a treasure who find Christ, a treasure of life. To open it up, I will shew,

1. What life they find who find Christ.

2. What are the qualities of this life.

First, I will shew what life they find who find Christ. It is a life that goes as wide as the death they found in Adam; Rom. v. 11, "For if through the offence of any one, many be dead; much more the grace of God, and the gift by grace, which is by one man, Jesus Christ, hath abounded unto many." It is a salve proportioned to that sore. The sinner's finding life in Christ implies, that without Christ, he is under death, which therefore we shall take along with us. And always the more of Christ, the more life; and the less of Christ, the less life. The sinner then finding Christ, finds,

1. A life of grace, in regeneration, which is a spiritual quickening of the soul; Eph. ii. 5, "Even when we were dead in sins, hath quickened us together with Christ." Man in his natural unconverted state, is spiritually dead, Eph. ii. 1. Adam eating the forbidden fruit, poisoned himself and all his offspring, for it brought immediate death to them; it separated them from God the fountain of life; and so they lie in their natural state, as buried in the grave of sin, void of all life and sense in spiritual things.

But in the day of the soul's finding Christ, the Spirit of Christ enters into it, and quickens it, as Lazarus's soul entering into his body, while Christ stood by his grave. So the dead soul is raised, the dry bones come together, and are made to live. The man is endowed with a new vital principle, putting him in a capacity to move and act graciously, Gal. ii. 20. He is a new creature, as one raised from the dead. There is a new light let into his mind, a new set given to his will, a new regulation made on his affections; all is new, as by a first resurrection.

2. A life of favour with God; Psalm xxx. 5, "In his favour is life." God is Lord of life and death, and we have forfeited our life to him by our rebellions. May not one say then, he is a dead man, who is out of God's favour; and he is secured for life, who enjoys it? A sinner out of Christ is a dead man, in so far as he is dead in law, and the broken law has doomed him to die eternally, Gal. iii. 10. All the fearful threats and curses of the first covenant, are twisted about him as so many cords of death, binding him as a condemned criminal, till the day of execution.

But the sinner finding Christ, the sentence of condemnation is reversed, he is no more a condemned man, Rom. viii. 1. Christ comes into the iron-house, makes a discovery of himself to the sinner in chains, and there the match is made betwixt the Bridegroom and the captive daughter of Zion. The prison-garments are taken off, and the marriage-robe is put on the believer, Phil. iii. 9. Then God says, "Deliver him from going down to the pit; I have found a ransom," Job xxxiii. 24. So the chains of guilt drop off, and the prison-doors are set open to Christ to hand out his spouse by, and the face-covering that was on the condemned is destroyed. Now, who has anything to say, why the prisoner may not go forth free with her Lord and Husband? Rom. viii. 33. Justice is satisfied, who had the claim against her; the law that laid her up, and kept her bound, has no more to demand, Gal. ii. 20. The debt is paid, the bond is got up, and torn in pieces, Col. ii. 14. The jailor therefore cannot keep her longer, and death which stood before her with a devouring mouth, is swallowed up in victory, Isa. xxv. 8.

3. A life of new obedience; Rom. vi. 4, "Therefore we are buried with him by baptism into death; that like as Christ was raised up from the dead by the glory of the Father, even so we also should walk in newness of life." By nature we are quite void of this life, John xv. 5. The soul in its natural state is never idle indeed, but ever working; but then all its works are dead works, Heb. ix. 14, which can never please the living God. The old man has his deeds in them that are out of Christ, and all their deeds are so; their very religious duties are dead works, and in them they are but as walking ghosts. They cannot perform one vital action in a spiritual sense; Gen. vi. 5, Psalm xiv. 3, Tit. i. 15.

But the sinner finding Christ finds newness of life. He is not the man he was. Christ not only brings him out of the grave of his natural state but he looses all his grave-clothes of reigning lusts, and sets him a-pulling them off, and casting them from him; Col. iii. 8. He gives them change of raiment. The man puts on Christ, personates him, walking as he also walked. Now his obedience is universal, Psalm cxix. 6; his heart is shaped out in breadth and length to the whole law of Christ. It is spiritual; it is a cluster of vital actions, whereof Christ is the principle; Gal. ii. 20, and the end Phil. i. 21.

4. A life of comfort. *Non vivere valere sed est vita*; 1 Sam. xxv. 6. 1 Thess. iii. 8. The natural man has the most uncomfortable life in the world. He has no solid ground of comfort, because matters are quite wrong betwixt Heaven and him; he has no actual comfort, but as it were in a dream, when he drinks of the broken cisterns, so as to forget his misery: Job xv. 21.

But the sinner finding Christ finds a life of comfort. He is put into a comfortable state, as reconciled to God, and having his sin pardoned; Psalm xxxii. 1. And if at any time he want comfort, it is not because the ground of it is rased, for that can never be while the everlasting covenant remains, 2 Sam. xxiii. 5, but because his eyes are held that he cannot perceive it, like Hagar at the well. And in his deepest sorrows and distress, there is a seed of comfort that will spring up; Psalm xcvii. 11. Light is sown for the righteous, and gladness for the upright in heart.

5. *Lastly*, Eternal life; John xvii. 3. Man in his natural state is a dead man, liable to eternal death in hell. And whosoever lives and dies in that state, cannot miss to perish for ever; Mark xvi. 16. Wherefore whenever God opens the sinner's eyes to see his own case, he sees he is eternally lost if he get not help; Acts ii. 37.

But the sinner finding Christ finds eternal life; John iii. *ult.* The second death can have no power over him, from that happy moment. He commences an heir of glory, and heaven's happiness is secured to him. Come death when it will, come judgment when it will, his happy state is already determined by the word, and can never be reversed.

Secondly, I shall shew what are the qualities of the life which they find who find Christ.

1. It is a divine life; Eph. iv. 18. So it is the most excellent life. The vegetative life, by which our bodies grow, is common to us with the plants of the earth; the life of sense, with brutes; the life of reason, with infidels; but this life exalts one to a rank of beings superior to the rest of mankind, namely, into the rank of saints partakers of the divine nature.

2. It is a life of the whole man. Sinners out of Christ are but half alive, and that in the worst half too, while their bodies are alive, their souls are dead within them; 1 Tim. v. 6. But on the soul's finding Christ, the soul is made alive too, and so the whole man lives; the better part is quickened. And as the dead souls of the wicked will secure the eternal death of their bodies too, death spreading itself from their souls to their bodies; so the life of the soul will secure the eternal life of the body, life spreading in like manner from the soul to the body; Rom. viii. 11.

3. It is a pleasant life; Prov. iii. 17. Sinners are generally prejudiced in the case, as if it were an unpleasant and uncomfortable life; but that is the opinion only of those who are unacquainted with it; for David could say, Psalm iv. 7, "Thou hast put gladness in my heart, more than in the time that their corn and their wine increased." It is true, the pleasure of it is not expressed in the noisy way in which the world expresses theirs; it is a water that runs deeper than to make such a noise as the shallow brooks and muddy streams of the world's pleasures do. But all the pleasantries of the men of the world, are light as a feather in comparison of the pleasure found in communion with God, the sense of his favour, and the serenity of conscience; by this good token, that these will bear up a man in the greatest distresses, where those others evanish at the blast; Hab. iii. 17.

4. It is a persevering life, that can never be lost; Hab. ii. 4, "The just shall live by his faith." Compare Heb. x. 38. It is a life that, from the moment it is given, shall never die out for ever; John iv. 14. The life of inherent grace may be very low, but can never be lost; one may lose the sense of the life of favour with God, but can never lose the thing itself; John v. 24. They that now lead the most honourable and wealthy life in the world, death will put an end to it; but this life will make its way through death itself, unhurt.

5. *Lastly*, It is a growing life; John x. 10. It is true, the Christian life is not always growing, more than the trees in winter. But it is a life that grows universally, regularly, and proportionably, till it come to its perfection in glory; Prov. iv. 18, "The path of the just is as the shining light, that shineth more and more unto the perfect day." It buds in regeneration, begins to open in progressive sanctification, and is full spread in glory; but it shall never wither, but be fresh and fragrant through eternity.

II. In order to confirm this doctrine, That sinners finding Christ find life, consider,

1. The Mediator, by the Father's appointment, is the immediate

receptacle of life for all to whom life is designed by the Father, Col. i. 19; as the bowl in Zechariah's candlestick received the oil from the two olive-trees, and communicated the same by the pipes to the lamps; Zech. iv. 2, 3. God seeing all mankind dead in Adam, but having destined the elect number to life, has put life for them all in the Mediator, as in a sure repository, where it cannot be lost; 1 John v. 11, hence the apostle draws the conclusion of our text; ver. 12, "He that hath the Son, hath life;" even as he who hath a woman in marriage, hath all that is hers; so he that hath Christ, not only hath a right to, but actually hath life, even everlasting life; ver. 13; John v. 24. He that buys the field hath the treasure in it.

2. As Adam lost his life, and that of all his posterity, by his losing of God, who is the life and soul of the soul of man; Psalm xxx. 5, in separation of the soul from whom its death lies; so the sinner finding Christ finds God again, and therefore must needs find life. God is in Christ, the fulness of the Godhead is in him; Col. ii. 9, and by him the believer comes to God; Heb. vii. 25, for that was the end of his death, "that he might bring us to God;" 1 Pet. iii. 18. The Father becomes his Father, the Son his Saviour, the Holy Ghost his Sanctifier; for a whole Trinity is made over to the sinner in the covenant "I am thy God." So finding Christ, the sinner finds the whole Trinity of persons; how then can he but find life?

3. The sinner finding Christ finds the Spirit of life. This is so certain, that "if any man have not the Spirit of Christ, he is none of his," Rom. viii. 9. Not only do the graces of the Spirit dwell in them who have found Christ, but the person of the Spirit, the cause of the other; Rom. viii. 11. This is that which gives them life, preserves it that it cannot be lost, increaseth it, and at length perfects it; John iv. 14. We see many who getting some light touches and common operations of the Spirit, seem to live for a while; but their seeming life wears away by degrees, and they never recover it; why? because not having found Christ, they have not found life, nor the Spirit either. But believers are recovered from their decays, because the Spirit of life still remains with them.

4. The sinner finding Christ, is united to him as a member of his body; Eph. iii. 17. Hence his life secures theirs; John xiv. 19, "Because I live, ye shall live also." They cannot die, as long as he lives, and therefore their life is everlasting. As members of Christ, the Spirit of Christ dwells in them, as the principle of their life; and they derive spiritual nourishment from him, as the branches from the vine-stock. Hence it is that the resurrection of their mortal bodies is secured to them, according to Rom. viii. 11, "But if the

Spirit of him that raised up Jesus from the dead, dwell in you; he that raised up Christ from the dead, shall also quicken your mortal bodies, by his Spirit that dwelleth in you." So that finding Christ, they find everlasting life of soul and body.

5. The sinner finding Christ, finds all the promises of the everlasting covenant, which are all promises of life, as the threatenings of the law are of death; Tit. i. 2; 2 Cor. i. 20; for the promises are immediately made to Christ; Gal. iii. 16, and in right of him they become ours. Hence "he that spared not his own Son, but delivered him up for us all, how shall he not with him also freely give us all things?" Rom. viii. 32. Some would reckon themselves made up all their life, if they did find a parcel of bank-bills; but he that finds Christ, finds heaven's bank-bills, which being presented to God, will get payment of them to the bearer, be who he will, and that such as will make him live happily through the ages of eternity.

6. The sinner finding Christ, finds a satisfactory answer to all the law's demands, which staves him off from life till they be satisfied. (1.) The law demands the debt of perfect obedience, if the sinner will have life; Matth. xix. 17. In Christ this is answered; for "Christ is the end of the law for righteousness to every one that believeth;" Rom. x. 4. (2.) It demands the debt of punishment, for satifaction of justice for sin done. The answer is, "I am crucified with Christ;" Gal. ii. 20. Thus he has found a complete righteousness, in which the law itself can find no blemish nor defect. Thus the current of death towards the believer is stopped, and the waters of the curse are dried up; and life flows into the soul, and the blessing comes in room of the curse.

7. *Lastly*, To sum up all in a word, The sinner finding Christ, finds all things necessary to make him happy. See the believer's possessions, what he gets with Christ when he gets him; 1 Cor. iii. 22, 23, "Whether Paul, or Apollos, or Cephas, or the world, or life, or death, or things present, or things to come; all are yours; and ye are Christ's; and Christ is God's." Rom. viii. 32, "He that spared not his own Son, but delivered him up for us all, how shall he not with him also freely give us all things?" There is a treasure in him, or he is a treasure, and the treasure becomes the believer's; Matth. xiii. 44. There are unsearchable riches in him, and they are all made over to the believer; Eph. iii. 8. Look to the whole of Christ's purchase, what he bought for poor sinners with his blood, and the soul finding Christ finds it all, and may say, It is all mine.

I shall now make some practical improvement of this branch of the text.

Use I. Of information. This informs us,

1. That the best way for one's security in an evil day, is to have found Christ. This is a day of impending wrath, wherein God is threatening to cause death overflow the nation.* The true way to answer God's call in the dispensation of the day, is to seek Christ, that ye may find him; so shall ye find life.

1st, God is threatening to take away men's substance, the means of life, making the heavens as brass, and the earth as iron.† He has locked up in great measure the pastures of the field, so that the beasts groan under the sins of men. And no wonder, considering the sinful improvement that has been made of their prosperity. But if all should go together, it cannot break the true Christian, who finding Christ has found life, and may say as Hab. iii. 17, 18, " Although the fig-tree shall not blossom, neither shall fruit be in the vines, the labour of the olive shall fail, and the fields shall yield no meat, the flock shall be cut off from the fold, and there shall be no herd in the stalls; yet I will rejoice in the Lord, I will joy in the God of my salvation."

2dly, God is threatening to make death ride in triumph among men. He has been sweeping away multitudes abroad; and how can these nations think to escape, nations lying under the fearful guilt of former times, and who have been long busied in filling up their cup to the brim? All ranks in church and in state have corrupted their ways; and when we consider the unnatural marriages, and unnatural murders, that have fallen out more than at any time ever I remember, I cannot but take them for presages, that the things which concern this generation are making haste, the hearing of which will make men's ears to tingle. Well, Sirs, happy are they that find Christ; for they shall find life, when death in its most frightful aspect shall seize a God-provoking generation, and make all their courage fail in one moment, never to recover.

2. There is no way to attain to holiness, and acceptable obedience in good works, without finding of Christ, or closing with him upon a saving discovery of him made to the soul. Find what we will, if we find not Christ, we will remain in a state of death; and all the reasons and motives that can be fetched from heaven or hell, will not quicken us; and therefore cannot put us upon the doing of the least good work; for, says Christ, " without me ye can do nothing," John xxv. 5. It is true, that, as, in an earthquake, dead bodies may fly from one place to another, by the force of commotion, yet still

---

* Referring to the plague which had then broke out in France, and proved very mortal in several places, particularly at Marseilles.

† This refers to a great drought in spring, 1721.

void of life; so an unbeliever, by the fear of punishment and hope of reward, may work, as one for his life; but alas! his works are but dead works still.

3. The true way to holiness is the finding of Jesus Christ; John vi. 28, 29, "Then said they unto him, What shall we do, that we might work the works of God? Jesus answered and said unto them, this is the work of God, that ye believe on him whom he hath sent." If ever ye would be holy, believe; if ye would reach the highway called the way of holiness, betake yourselves to him who is the way, and the truth, and the life; John xiv. 6. As the dead man (2 Kings xiii. 21,) let down into Elisha's grave, as soon as he touched the bones of Elisha, revived, and stood up on his feet; so the dead soul meeting with Christ by participation of his Spirit is quickened. And as a wick put to a burning lamb is lighted, so as immediately they join flames, and burn on; so the soul finding Christ finds life, embraces him, and lives by him and to him.

4. Christ does not set his people to work for life, to procure life to themselves by their own working; he has given them life, a life that will never end, in their union with them, and bids them work from that life. The law or covenant of works says to them who are under it, Do this, and live; if ye will have life, work and win it; Matth. xix. 17. But Christ says to the poor tired creature, busy at labour in vain, Come to me that you may have life. And having come and received life, he sets it to work.

5. Faith and obedience are inseparable; John xv. 5, "He that abideth in me, and I in him, the same bringeth forth much fruit." Rom. vi. 14, "Sin shall not have dominion over you; for ye are not under the law, but under grace." The life that sinners find, finding Christ is without question, for the kind of it, a holy life; and the manner of one's working must needs be of a piece with the manner of one's being. When Nebuchadnezzar was driven from men to herd with the beasts of the field, he lived like the beasts. Men living in sin, walk in it; Col. iii. 7. And those who are blessed with a life that is holy in the nature of it, must needs be holy in their walk; and if that life were perfected, they would be perfectly holy. So where there is no holiness, there is no life, no faith, no union with the holy Jesus. Unholy professors are dead sinners, and will be buried out of sight in the pit; Heb. xii. 14, "Without holiness no man shall see the Lord."

6. *Lastly*, The one thing we have to seek above all things, for time and eternity, is to find Christ. For whoso findeth him findeth life, for time and eternity. And this is not the work only of the time

of our first conversion to God, but the work of our whole lives, 1 Pet. ii. 4, compared with vers. 2, 3. For always the more we find of Christ, we have the more life, and the less of him, the less life. Finding Christ we find all for holiness and happiness. The Jews say, that the 613 precepts of the law are all reduced to this saying, Hab. ii. 4, "The just shall live by his faith." And the truth is, the sum of the Christian life lies here; Gal. ii. 20,

Use. II. Of exhortation. Seek Christ until ye find him, and find life in him and by him. To press this, I offer the following motives.

Motive 1. Man is a seeking creature: Matth. xiii. 45. Sinners out of Christ are as busy seeking as others are, like the watch going as fast when wrong as when right. There is a void within that would be filled; but the matter is, they go all wrong in their search. They are seeking a rest to their hearts in the creature, and a rest to their conscience in the works of the law; but in neither of these will they find what they seek. Turn ye, sinners, seek Christ; why seek ye the living among the dead? In Christ only is to be found what ye are seeking, rest to the conscience and to the heart.

Motive 2. Now is the time he is to be found; Isa. lv. 6. The day will come when he will not be to be found; and so the sinner has no more access to life. Remember the case of the foolish virgins; Matth. xxv. That is a heavy word; Prov. i. 24, 26, "Because I have called, and ye refused, I have stretched out my hand, and no man regarded;—I also will laugh at your calamity, I will mock when your fear cometh." And how stinging will it then be to think, that the time of seeking Christ was spent in seeking what cannot profit; and that then all access to him is lost for ever.

Motive ult. Ye will be made up for ever, if ye find Christ; and undone, if ye find him not; Prov. viii. 35, 36. If one was taken up all the days of his life, seeking him, and should find him at last, all would be found to be well bestowed; Matth. xiii. 45, 46. And find what we will, if we should find all the wealth, honours, and pleasures of the world, it would not compensate the loss of a missed Saviour; Matth. xvi. 26. But I will branch out this exhortation in two particulars.

First, Sinners, seek to find Christ, and to find life in him, by getting a saving discovery of him made to your souls. To press seeking of this saving discovery, consider,

Mot. 1. There is no closing with Christ, or believing in him, without a saving discovery of him made to the soul; Psalm ix. 10; John iv. 10. Men may believe in an unseen, but not an unknown Christ. There is an illumination in the knowledge of Christ, that is necessary towards the embracing of him. Without it the wounded soul will pine away in its wounds, not knowing the Physician; and the sinner in his sins, not knowing the Saviour.

2. All your labour in religion, without this, will be but working in the dark, and labour in vain; John xiv. 6, compared with Eccl. x. 15. What will all attainments in religion avail, without the knowledge of the main thing, *i. e.* the knowledge of Christ? Matth. vii. 22, we find some prophesying in Christ's name, in his name casting out devils, and in his name doing many wonderful works, who lose all their pains, because there was no saving acquaintance betwixt Christ and them.

3. The discovery of Christ is the most excellent discovery that men are capable of. Therefore Paul determined to seek after nothing but that; 1 Cor. ii. 2; he preferred it to all other things; Phil. iii. 8. What though men be ever so well acquainted with the nature of the creation, and can dive into the secret mysteries of nature, with the reasons of the same? if they be unacquainted with Christ, it is but a bewitching vanity, and a gilded ignorance.

The knowledge of Christ appears to be the most noble, if one considers, (1.) The superlative excellency of the object; Col ii. 9, " In him dwelleth all the fulness of the Godhead bodily." (2.) The way and manner one comes to this knowledge. Not by the light of nature; this cannot discover Christ to a soul; not by mere objective revelation in the word; men may indeed learn much of Christ that way, but may go to hell for it all; but by the light of the Spirit and subjective revelation; Matth. xvi. 16, 17. (3.) The certainty of it, which surpasses all demonstration; Heb. xi. 1. (4.) The usefulness of it. Other knowledge men may have, and perish with it; all the arts and sciences in the world cannot give life to the soul; but this is life, eternal life to them that have it; John xvii. 3. Wherefore all other researches are but laborious trifling, unless in so far as they are subservient to this.

4. Christ discovered in his glory will satisfy your souls, and arrest your hearts; Matth. xiii. 45, 46, " Be shut my eyes and ears," saith Luther, " and say, you know no God out of Christ, none but he that was in the lap of Mary, and sucked her breasts." What is the reason of the apostasy and backsliding of many, but that they were never brought into this inner court of religion? If they had, they had been held fast. They had seen in him what is fully commensurate to the desires of a soul, and therefore had no occasion to have gone back unto the world and their lusts. This would be an anchor of the soul, in the midst of temptations, troubles, persecutions, and losses, arising from whatever quarter they may; and is the absolutely best way to fix the heart.

5. Christ is a vailed beauty, an unknown Christ to the most part of the hearers of the Gospel, and to all those to whom the Holy Spirit has not given saving illumination, Cant. v. 9, compare John i. 10. Beware he continue not to be so unto you. Seek to get the vail removed, that ye may see that in Christ, which the world left to perish in their iniquity never sees. The leading difference betwixt the wise and the foolish builders, and the wise and the foolish virgins was, the one had illumination, the other had not.

6. *Lastly*, Without a saving discovery of Christ, ye perish, John xvii. 3. Isa. liii. 11. Ignorance of, and unacquaintedness with Christ must needs be fatal to the soul, since he is the only way to the Father, and there is no salvation in any other. It is the great design of the Gospel to bring souls acquainted with Jesus Christ; so where that is not reached, the gospel has not its effect ; and where the gospel has not a saving effect, the law will take effect to one's condemnation.

I shall give you some directions for obtaining this discovery of Christ.

DIRECTION 1. Labour to be acquainted with yourselves, your own sinfulness and misery. And for that cause lay your hearts, lives, and state, to the rule of the holy law. Conviction leads the way to saving illumination, the knowledge of the disease to that of the physician, Acts xvi. 30, 31.

2. Seek the discovery of Christ in your attendance on public ordinances, Prov. viii. 34. These are the galleries where the king walks, the lattices by which he shews himself. See Psalm xlv. 8. There is the market where the eye-salve is to be bought of him. There Lydia's heart was opened. It is good to be in Christ's way, as Zaccheus was. And were we looking and longing for a discovery of him there, we would not long want it.

3. Seek the discovery of him in his written word, the scriptures, for they are they which testify of Christ, John v. 39. God's word is the great means of illumination; Psalm xix. 8. The Psalmist found it to be so by experience, Psalm cxix. 130, " The entrance of thy words giveth light; it giveth understanding unto the simple." It is the special instrument the Spirit uses for illumination.

4. Seek it earnestly in prayer, Prov. ii. 3—5. When the disciples were together at prayer, the doors being shut, he manifested himself unto them. We are not to expect bodily discoveries of Christ; if we had them, they would not do our turn; the Jews saw him so who believed not on him; but we are to seek a discovery of Christ in the glory of his person and offices, by the Spirit, which alone can be attended with saving effects.

5. *Lastly.* Whenever the Lord lets in the least beam of heavenly

light into your souls, cherish it, though it may be painful by discovering your sin and misery; make much of it; after little, more may come, Hos. vi. 3.

Secondly, Seek to find Christ and life in him, by getting an interest in him. The soul then finds Christ, and has life, when it has got an interest in him. If you enquire how that interest is got? It is through faith. God hath given to us eternal life in the free offer of the gospel, and that life is in his Son, 1 John v. 11. Believe the word of the gospel with particular application to yourselves, receive and rest on him siducially for life, the life of grace and glory, and ye have it. Wherefore come to Christ, that ye may have life. To press this, consider,

MOTIVE 1. Ye are to come to Christ, that ye may get life in and by him, Isa. lv. 1, 2, "Ho, every one that thirsteth, come ye to the waters, and he that hath no money; come ye, buy and eat, yea, come, buy wine and milk without money, and without price. Wherefore do ye spend money for that which is not bread? and your labour for that which satisfieth not? hearken diligently unto me, and eat ye that which is good, and let your soul delight itself in fatness." Rev. iii. 20, "Behold, I stand at the door and knock; if any man hear my voice, and open the door I will come in to him, and will sup with him, and he with me." Here is an invitation to life, let not that complaint be made of you, John v. 40, "Ye will not come to me, that ye might have life." Consider,

1st, It is an offer the fallen angels never got. When Christ was born there was good-will towards men, but no sign of it towards fallen angels. Yet they are in themselves a rank of beings superior to mankind, and he owed no more to us than to them. Only his sovereign pleasure made the difference. "How then shall we escape, if we neglect so great salvation?"

2dly, It is an invitation not given to millions in the world, who are the sons of Adam as well as we. Many kingdoms and empires in the world lie in darkness and the shadow of death, and no offer of life is made to them; but it is made to you.

3dly, It is the greatest offer that ever was or shall be, that heaven can give and earth receive, admired by angels, and grudged by devils; and shall it be slighted by men? even an offer of the son of God, and eternal life in him.

4thly, It is an offer frequently repeated. Now sinner, Christ is boding himself and eternal life upon you. You have given him many refusals, but he will not yet take your refusal, but continues the offer.

MOTIVE 2. Christ is very willing to give himself, and eternal life in himself to you, John vi. 37. Consider,

1st, How ample and large the gospel offer is, excluding none that will come, Isa. lv. 1, forecited. Rev. xxii. 17, " Whosoever will, let him take the water of life freely."

2dly, There is no case a sinner can be in, that shall mar his reception with Christ, and partaking of life, if he will come to Christ; Isa. i. 18, " Come now, and let us reason together, saith the Lord; though your sins be as scarlet, they shall be as white as snow ; though they be red like crimson, they shall be as wool." Manasseh's bloodshed and witchcraft, Paul's blasphemy and persecution, and Mary Magdalene's lewdness, hindered not their getting life in and by Christ. When he was in the world, he raised Lazarus when sinking in the grave, as well as the ruler's daughter newly dead.

3dly, He takes kindly notice of the sinner's first steps towards him; the father met the prodigal son while yet a great way of See Jer. xxxi. 18—20. He surprises souls with looks of kindness preventing them, Is. lxv. 1, as he did Paul, Zaccheus, and others.

4thly, He is at great pains with sinners to bring them to himself for life. He stands and knocks; by convictions, surprising mercies, rods, and crosses, he says in effect, " Why will ye die ?"

Motive 3. Ye are commanded to come to him, that ye may have life ; 1 John iii. 23, " This is his commandment, that we should believe on the name of his Son Jesus Christ." All the gospel invitations are commands ; so that it is not left to you whether to come or not; but ye are peremptorily enjoined. Consider,

1st, Ye are creatures owing obedience to the commands of your sovereign Lord; and therefore trample not on his gospel command.

2dly, How highly merciful and reasonable this command is. All God's commandments are most righteous, Psalm cxix. 128. But behold this is an eminently merciful and reasonable one, that the creature should seek the favour of its Creator; that man should be at peace with God ; that the poor sinner should go to the rich Saviour, the sick to the Physician, the guilty flee to the city of refuge and live, and the dying soul have recourse to the fountain of life. And all this under the pain of God's displeasure.

3dly, What a mercy it is that there is not a countermand; that when Adam and his offspring fell, God did not forbid them ever to hope for the least grain of mercy; but graciously invites and intreats, yea, and commands them to come and partake of his favour!

4thly, It is such a command, that if it be not obeyed, God has no value for all other obedience, 1 John iii. 23, John vi. 29.

Mot. 4. Ye need Christ, and ye need life; ye have an absolute need of both. Do ye not need grace, the favour of God, pardon of sin, the light of his countenance, the influences of his Spirit, the manifestations of his love? Without these ye can never be happy, but eternally miserable. O then seek to find Christ, and life in him.

Use. *Ult.* Hereby ye may try whether ye have found Christ or not. The soul yet dead in sin hath not found him; but where there is spiritual life, Christ is found by that soul. How shall one know whether he be spiritually dead or alive? I will offer but three marks.

Mark 1. Spiritual light, not only let into the conscience, but into the heart, 2 Cor. iv. 6, John viii. 12. And that may be known by these two things.

(1.) The discovery it makes. The light of life shews a man his former darkness, making him say, "Once was I blind, but now I see." It discovers sin in its sinfulness, not only as dangerous, but as loathsome and abominable; the sinfulness of heart-sins as well as of life-sins; the first movings of sin, as well as of sin ripened by consent or action; the man's own utter inability to help himself, and the need of Christ both for justification, and sanctification; Christ's preciousness, and perfect suitableness to the sinner's case. This is the discovery made by the light of life, or saving illumination, Luke xv. 17, 1 Pet. ii. 17.

(2.) The efficacy it hath on the soul, Matth. iii. 11. There are many who have a great deal of light; but it has no more efficacy on them to bring them from sin to holiness, than painted fire has to burn. But the light of life humbles the soul before God; causes grief for sin and hatred of of it, as contrary to God's holy nature and will; a holy despairing of help by ourselves or any other creature; and a betaking one's self to Christ for all, for pardon, and favour with God, for holiness and happiness, Phil. iii. 3.

Mark 2. Where there is spiritual life there is spiritual sense and feeling. In spiritual death all the senses of the soul, so to speak, are locked up; and they may be at some times very dull in those who are spiritually alive. But it is evident, that in the quickening of the soul they are restored, and never lost again altogether. The eyes of the soul are opened to see God, Christ, sin, the world, and all things that concern the soul, in other colours than formerly. They hear his voice in his word and in his rod, and they discern it from all others, Cant. v. 2, so that their great business is to answer his call. They have tasted that the Lord is gracious; they have the witness in themselves, that there is something in religion more desirable than all the profits and pleasures of the world, John v. 10. They can say from their experience, that all his garments smell of myrrh, aloes, and cassia, Psalm xlv. 8, that everything about Christ is lovely and desirable. The fulness of grace lodged in him, is savoury to them, Cant. i. 3. Their sense of feeling is awakened; the burden of sin they sometime went lightly under, makes them groan now, and long to be rid of it, as ever a poor prisoner was of his chains; Rev. vii. 24, "O wretched man that I am, who shall deliver me from the body of this death?" Every limb of that body is a weight to them. And they are sensible of Christ's goings and comings, his hidings and manifestations of himself, and the power of his grace; Psalm xxx. 7, "Lord, by thy favour thou hast made my mountain to stand strong; thou didst hide thy face, and I was troubled."

MARK 3. Where there is spiritual life, there is a kindly heat and warmth of the same kind. There is a threefold flame kindled in the believer in the day of his being restored to life, though it acts not alike vigorously in all, nor in the same person alike at all times.

(1.) There is a flame of holy desires; Isa. xxvi. 9. They have longing desires after righteousness, both imputed and implanted; Matth. v. 6, they are set for the one as well as the other. They have ardent desires after communion with God in Christ; Psalm xlii. 1. Hence the secret cries of the soul, O that I knew where I might find him! O when wilt thou come unto me!

(2.) There is a flame of love to Christ; Rom. v. 5. They love him above all persons and things; Luke xiv. 26. They love his truths, his whole word; his commands, though striking against their corruptions; Rom. vii. 22, his promises, as the sweetest cordials to a soul fainting under the apprehensions of wrath, or prevailing of corruption; the threatening of his word approving them heartily as most just; Rom. vii. 12. Their hearts warm to any in whom God's image appears, and that because of that image; 1 John iii. 14. They love his ordinances; Psalm lxxxiv. 1, because they are his institutions, and the appointed means of communion with him.

(3.) There is a flame of zeal for Christ; Psalm lxix. 9. They are concerned for his honour in the world, the thriving of his kingdom. It vents itself in indignation against sin in themselves and others, because of the dishonour it reflects on Christ; 2 Cor. vii. 11, in endeavouring to be active for God in their station, and grieving for the ills which they cannot help, saying with David, "Rivers of waters run down mine eyes, because they keep not thy law," Psalm cxix. 136.

SINNERS INTERESTED IN CHRIST, OBTAINING FAVOUR OF THE LORD.

Proverbs viii. 35,

Whoso findeth me,—shall obtain favour of the Lord.

By the favour of the Lord is not meant reconciliation, or a state of favour with God, for that is comprehended in the life found; but the benefits, fruit, and effects of God's favour, all along from the time the sinner is taken into favour. The word rendered obtained, signifies to bring forth as out of a treasure or storehouse. This treasure is open to the sinner, and access to it granted him, upon his union with Christ, so that from thence he may afterwards bring forth as he needs.

The doctrine deducible from the words is,

DOCTRINE. A sinner once interested in Christ, shall obtain favour of the Lord, bringing it forth as out of a treasure to which he is allowed access.

In handling this point, I shall,

1. Shew some things supposed in this truth, tending to clear the meaning of it.

II. Wherein the soul once interested in Christ shall obtain favour of the Lord.

III. Confirm the doctrine.

IV. Apply.

I. I will shew some things supposed in this truth, tending to clear the meaning of it.

1. There is a treasure of favour for poor sinners with the Lord; Matth. xiii. 44, "The kingdom of heaven is like unto treasure hid in a field," &c. A treasure speaks preciousness, variety, and abundance. God's favours are precious, because of his infinite excellency; there is a variety of them, suited to all the cases the sinner can be in; and there is abundance of them, an inexhaustible stock, sufficient to supply them all, and that at all times.

2. This treasure is locked on sinners out of Christ, they have no access to it, being aliens from the commonwealth of Israel, and strangers from the covenants of promise, having no hope, and without God in the world, Eph. ii. 12. There is favour with God, but it is not for such sinners; the treasure of wrath is their treasure, Rom. ii. 5. They have no saving interest in the Mediator, therefore no saving interest in the treasure of favour. It is hid in the field of the gospel; but the field is not theirs, so not the treasure neither.

3. The sinner once interested in Christ has free access to the treasure, to bring forth from thence whatever he needs; hence says the apostle, Heb. iv. 14, 16, "Seeing then that we have a great High Priest, that is passed into the heavens, Jesus the Son of God, —let us therefore come boldly unto the throne of grace, that we may obtain mercy, and find grace to help in time of need. But it may be objected, Is there not free access to that treasure of favour proclaimed to all to whom the gospel comes? Answ. It is so. But we may conceive, as it were, a twofold door of this treasure; the outer door, in the free offer of the gospel, the inner door, even Jesus Christ himself. Both are closed on fallen angels; the outer door is opened to sinners of the tribe of Adam, that they may freely partake of it, if they will come in by the inner door; but till they enter by this last, they cannot reach it. But the sinner once interested in Jesus Christ is put in possession of the treasure, so as to have access to it at any time thereafter, when he is disposed to bring forth favour out of it; John x. 9, "I am the door: by me if any man enter in, he shall be saved, and shall go in and out, and find pasture."

4. Even the sinner when he is interested in Christ, will still be needing, while he is in this world. It is true, he will never be again reduced to the extremity of total want, John iv. 14, but he will be under partial wants while he lives here, John xiii. 10. And there is such an emptiness woven into the very nature of the creature, that the saints in heaven, though they will feel no want, yet will not become self-sufficient by glorification.

5. *Lastly.* As it is the privilege of believers, that they may, so it is their duty that they do, bring forth and fetch supply for all their wants out of that treasure. They must still have recourse to it, in all exigencies; and they are welcome to it. They are let into it, by their union with Christ, and they should make use of it in their daily walk. And when they come to heaven, they shall be filled from it for evermore, Rev. vii. 17, "For the Lamb which is in the midst of the throne, shall feed them, and shall lead them unto living fountains of waters: and God shall wipe away all tears from their eyes."

II. I proceed to shew wherein the soul once interested in Christ shall obtain favour of the Lord. They shall obtain it in all things, cases, and conditions, which they meet with or shall be in. The promise is broad and large, Heb. xiii. 5, "I will never leave thee, nor forsake thee." Rom. viii. 28, "All things shall work together for good to them that love God, to them that are the called according to his purpose." Go as it will with the nation, the church, or themselves in particular, they shall always obtain favour. But it will not be amiss to condescend on some particulars. They shall obtain favour,

1. In prosperity, when things in the world are in a thriving condition with them. That is what destroys many, Prov. i. *ult.* but it shall not destroy them, and that is a great favour; Job i. 10, "Hast not thou made an hedge about him, and about his house, and about all that he hath upon every side?" a hedge not only about his house, &c., but about him. Many have the former, while they want the latter, and so are ruined. There is a threefold favour that a gracious person may obtain of the Lord in this case.

(1.) Balancing grace, to make them carry evenly and usefully in prosperity. Job got it in his prosperity, chap. i. 5. The sun of prosperity shone on him, and he was helped of God to retain his tenderness, and to improve the smiles of outward providences to the honour of God. And considering what a corrupt nature the best have, and how slippery ground the world's heights are, they obtain favour of the Lord indeed, whom Satan gets not cast over that precipice to their ruin.

(2.) Balancing providences, some such mixture of bitterness in their cup, as keeps them from miskenning themselves, and makes them sing of mercy and judgment; as the apostle experienced in his own case; 2 Cor. xii. 7, "And lest I should be exalted above measure through the abundance of the revelations, there was given to me a thorn in the flesh, the messenger of Satan to buffet me, lest I should be exalted above measure." It is no small favour to the Christian to have some thorn of uneasiness put under him while he is here, to keep him from lying down among the lions' dens and mountains of leopards, and sleeping in these dangerous places. Every rub a Christian meets with in his way through the world, is a memorandum for him, that "this is not his rest." If that do not prevail, there is,

(3.) The change of the course of providence into adversity. Many times that is as great a favour as a Christian can meet with; Zeph. iii. 12, " I will also leave in the midst of thee an afflicted and poor people, and they shall trust in the name of the Lord." Sometimes the Christian begins to feather his nest, and lie secure and forgetful of God; but God sets fire to his nest, and he is obliged to look to God whom he had forgotten. The world grows a burden to him, and God raises a wind that blows the burden off his back. And he draws away some gilded earth from him, that was drawing his heart from God.

2. In personal outward afflictions, to which the people of God

are liable as well as others. O it is a sad case with Christless sinners, under affliction: they cry out under their trouble, but they are not bettered by it; Job xxxv. 9, 10. Nay, many are worsted by their afflictions, their spirits are embittered; they have no comfort from earth, and they have none, and apply for none from heaven. But the sinner once interested in Christ shall obtain favour in this case.

(1.) They shall be bettered by it; Rom. viii. 28, forecited. Though they may for a time be fruitless under affliction, and as a bullock unaccustomed to the yoke, yet they shall be brought to themselves, and gain some spiritual advantage thereby. And that is no small favour, to gather figs of such thorns and briers.

(2.) They shall be supported under it; Isa. xliii. 2, "When thou passest through the waters, I will be with thee; and through the rivers, they shall not overflow thee; when thou walkest through the fire, thou shalt not be burnt; neither shall the flame kindle upon thee." Though with one hand they be cast down, they shall be held up with the other. They have fatherly pity and sympathy in all their afflictions, Isa. lxiii. 9, and in their hopeless case the everlasting arms are underneath them.

(3.) They shall have deliverance in due time, one way or other, that they shall not perish in their affliction. Though the night be ever so long, the morning cometh; the days of their mourning shall end; Psalm xxxiv. 19, "Many are the afflictions of the righteous; but the Lord delivereth him out of them all."

3. In desertion. Christ's spouse may be under desertion; the Lord may withdraw and hide himself from those that are dear to him; they may for a time "walk in darkness, and see no light;" Isa. l. 10, "go mourning without the sun," and be so pressed that they cannot contain themselves from crying out; Job xxx. 28. All communication betwixt heaven and them may seem to be stopt and blocked up; Lam. iii. 8. They may be under fearful terrors from the Lord; Job vi. 4. And this case may be of long continuance with them, as in Heman; Psalm lxxxviii. 15, "I am afflicted and ready to die, from my youth up; while I suffer thy terrors, I am distracted." But in such a case they shall obtain favour of the Lord.

(1.) They shall never be totally deserted or forsaken. Though the husband may withdraw, yet the relation shall never be broken, nor shall they go out of mind with him, though they may apprehend themselves to be forgotten; Isa. xlix. 14, 15, 16. They shall have now and then some gleam of light in their darkness, and a secret support shall never be wanting; Psalm cxii. 4; Deut. xxxiii. 27.

(2) They shall not be finally deserted; Isa. liv. 6. Though he may be gone, he will certainly return. There is a seed of joy sown, which though it lie never so long under the clod, it cannot rot, it will spring up; Psalm xcvii. 11. And for the spirit of heaviness they shall get the oil of joy. And the ill reports which unbelief has spread concerning a trying, hiding God, shall be proved false.

4. In temptation. While they are in the world, they are in a place of snares and temptations. Sometimes public temptations are going, compliance with which being fashionable it is hard to stand the shock. Private temptations are never wanting from a busy devil, an ensnaring world, and an evil heart. These are means of remediless ruin unto many. But in such a case they shall obtain favour of the Lord. They shall either,

1. Be made to keep their ground against the temptation, and stand conquerors; 2 Cor. xii. 9. They shall have grace to discover the snare, and grace to withstand the solicitations to comply with it. And that is a great favour bestowed on poor, weak, self-emptied Christians, in whom grace from the treasure of favour does triumph; while others leaning to themselves are suffered to fall; Isa. xl. 30, 31. The truth is there is no temptation so contemptible, but it will lay a self-confident man on his back; and none so great, but by faith the weakest Christian may get over it; Phil. iv. 13. I can do all things through Christ which strengtheneth me.

(2.) At least temptation shall not get a complete victory over them as over unbelievers; Luke xxii. 31, 32, "And the Lord said, Simon, Simon, behold, Satan hath desired to have you, that he may sift you as wheat; but I have prayed for thee, that thy faith fail not." Satan carried Peter far, even to the denying of Christ; but yet he found favour, that he could not get him all the length he would have had him. They may fall deep in temptation, but they will not be suffered to drown; for the Lord upholdeth them with his hand, Psalm xxxvii. 24.

5. Even when fallen into sin, the Lord will not leave them, nor cast them off; Heb. xiii. 5. They grieve the Spirit by their falls; so they may expect in that case, that God will withdraw the light of his countenance, that he will set a mark of his indignation upon their way, and it may cost them broken bones ere they recover. Yet in this case they shall obtain favour of the Lord.

(1.) God will not suffer them to lie still in it, but will raise them up again, John viii. 35. Some fall off, and are never recovered; but as for believers, not one of them shall be lost. God's love to them is through Jesus Christ; and forasmuch as he is always beloved of the Father, they shall ever be loved for his sake, Psalm lxxxix. 30—33. And love is active to raise up the beloved party fallen.

(2.) While he raiseth them up, he will make their falls work for good, Rom. viii. 28. Out of the eater shall be brought forth meat, and out of the strong sweetness. Satan shall be outshot in his own bow. They shall thereby be let into a clearer view of the corruption of their nature, see more need of Christ and his grace, be more emptied of themselves, and learn to prize imputed righteousness more, and so be led more to a life of faith, and close dependence on the Lord.

6. In a time of public calamity. We have all reason to look for such a time on this guilty declining generation, that God will sum up the old and new debts of Scotland, and charge them together upon the generation that is filling up the measure of our fathers. But come what will come, they that are once interested in Christ, shall obtain favour of the Lord.

(1.) It may be they shall be hid, and kept out of trouble, that the stroke shall not reach them, Zeph. ii. 3. The floods may swell, yet he that sitteth on the floods can keep them from touching his own when he will; and often does so, Psalm xxxii. 6, "Surely in the floods of great waters, they shall not come nigh unto him. Whatever be the stroke that is sent, every arrow has its commission, and can touch none whom God will have safe, Psalm xci. 7; as in the cases of Noah and Lot.

(2.) If it do fall upon them, they may expect a gracious mixture of favour in it; Jer. xv. 11, "The Lord said, Verily it shall be well with thy remnant, verily I will cause the enemy to entreat thee well in the time of evil and in the time of affliction. And the Lord has often made his care of his people in common calamity, with the beautiful mixture of kindnesses with sharp trials, more desirable in the issue, than to have been kept quite free, Rom. v. 3. This made Paul take a pleasure in distresses, 2 Cor. xii. 10.

(3.) Though it should come to an extremity with the child of God, yet the sting shall be out of it, and so it shall do him no real harm. Death is the worst of it, but the child of God may meet it with that saying; 1 Cor. xv. 55, "O death, where is thy sting? O grave, where is thy victory?" The truth is, whereas the blessings of the wicked are cursed, the curses are changed into blessings to them that are in Christ, Rom. viii. 28.

7. *Lastly*. At death, and through all the ages of eternity. During life the wicked receive many common favours from the Lord, but at death that spring is quite dried up to them. But then the spring of favour to them that are in Christ, never to be interrupted any more, begins to flow abundantly. They shall obtain favour of the Lord.

(1.) They shall then be perfectly freed from sin, and all inclination or temptation to it, Heb. xii. 23. They will then get a full answer to that petition, " Lead us not into temptation." The leprosy in the house will then be quite removed, when it is pulled down. And the body of sin shall breathe out its last with the death of the body.

(2.) They shall be freed from all trouble whatever, and enjoy perfect happiness in the full enjoyment of God, Rev. xiv. 13. At the last day their bodies shall obtain the favour of a blessed resurrection, and soul and body shall be eternally glorified together.

III. I shall next confirm the doctrine, That a sinner once interested in Christ, shall obtain favour of the Lord. This is evident, if ye consider,

1. They have a right to the whole treasure of favour through Jesus Christ, in whom they are interested; 1 Cor. iii. 22, 23, " All are yours; and ye are Christ's." It is the purchase of his precious blood, and a purchase made for them; and hence not only the love and mercy of God, but the justice of God secures their enjoyment of it, 2 Thess. i. 6, 7.

2. Jesus Christ is the dispenser of the treasure, the high Steward of the house of heaven. As he has purchased it by his blood, so the Father has put the dispensing or distributing of it in his hand, John v. 22, Matth. xxviii. 18. Now he is their best friend, yea, he is their husband, their head, and they are members of his body. How then can they miss of obtaining favour of the Lord.

3. The enjoyment of it is secured to them by the covenant of promises. In the covenant there are promises suited to every case they can be in; all these are " yea and amen in Christ." So being interested in Christ, they are interested in all the promises, 2 Pet. i. 4. These are the several articles of their marriage covenant with Christ, by which the whole treasure of the favour of God is settled upon Christ's espoused ones, for their throughbearing in time, and complete provision to all eternity.

4. *Lastly*. They have each of them a private key to the treasure, and that is faith; hence says our Lord, Matth. xxi. 22, " All things whatsoever ye shall ask in prayer, believing, ye shall receive." There is a cloud of witnesses, Heb. xi., who did, and suffered great things; not by their own strength, but by furniture from heaven; and how did they obtain it, but by faith, that self-emptying, taking, receiving grace, out of Christ's fulness? They who can rightly manage this key, need never want, be their case as low as it can be; faith is a noble provider, bringing strength to the weak, light to the blind, food to the hungry, clothing to the naked, &c.

I shall shut up this doctrine with some improvement.

Use I. Of information. It informs us, that,

1. Jesus Christ is the way to the Father, and the only way, John xiv. 6. Whoso would obtain favour of the Lord, must make him their friend in the first place. For he is the one Mediator, and all communication that we have with Heaven must be by him. They who place their confidence of acceptance with God in their duties, will obtain indignation and wrath, instead of favour from the Lord. For in Christ only God is or can be well pleased with one that is a sinful creature.

2. Those who are interested in Christ are made up for ever, their bread is baken for time and eternity. They are provided for all conditions they can be in, or circumstances they can be brought into. This is a plentiful treasure, and a treasure that has no bottom, which is made over to them in Christ. Alas! that ever any losses in the world should disquiet a believer, that "has in heaven a better and an enduring substance," Heb. x. 34. He may put his gain in Christ in the balance with all worldly losses, and it will weigh them all down.

3. Those who are without Christ are without the favour of God, Eph ii. 12. Common favours they may receive, but special favour is far from them. The truth is, the best things they get are blasted to them; hence their prosperity destroys them, and the very gospel of God is the savour of death. How can they have the favour of a holy just God, who are not reconciled to him in his Son, and clothed with his righteousness?

4. *Lastly.* It is believers' own fault, that at any time they are not sufficiently provided according as their case requires. They may have it for the bringing it forth out of the treasure, John i. 16. The breasts are full, if we would suck of the divine consolations. The armoury is sufficiently furnished for the spiritual warfare, if we could bring forth the weapons. The promises which the believer is interested in, are the channel of conveyance of supply; but alas! faith is often wanting, which should draw it in through these means of conveyance. If we could believe, all things would be possible.

Use II. Of exhortation, both to sinners and saints. And,

First, To sinners. Labour ye above all things to get an interest in Christ. O that I could engage you to this pursuit! Truly this is and ought to be made by you the great business of your life, the great interest ye are to pursue, John vi. 29. Ye are all pursuing some one interest or other; and carnal worldly interest is what has the greatest number of followers. I would exhort you to labour to secure an interest in Christ. To press this, consider,

Motive 1. An interest in Christ is the most worthy interest ye can pursue. And I would commend it to you as such, as deserving your highest esteem and regard, as far excelling all the low and secular interests that can possibly engage your attention. It is the one thing needful, in comparison of which all other pursuits are arrant trifles.

MOTIVE 2. It is an interest that ye may now obtain. Christ is willing to be yours, and to confer upon you his whole fulness, all the riches of his grace and glory. "Behold, now is the accepted time: behold, now is the day of salvation." "To-day, if ye will hear the voice of Christ speaking in the gospel, harden not your hearts." Christ now calls you to come to him, that ye may have an interest in him. O then for the Lord's sake, and your own souls' sake, delay not to come to him, that ye may have life, and obtain favour of the Lord.

Secondly, To saints. Labour ye to improve your interest in Christ, by bringing in to yourselves daily out of that treasure for whatsoever ye need. The treasure is opened to you, ye are allowed free access to it; improve your privilege by bringing forth out of it suitable supply for all your wants.

QUEST. But how is that to be done? what way can one bring forth supply out of the treasure of favour? *Ans.* By faith. Faith is the key of the treasure-door that opens it, the feet that carry into it, the hand of the soul that takes up the necessary supply, and brings it away, Heb. xi. Hence the believer is said to "live by faith," Gal ii. 20, it being that which by its communication with Christ maintains the spiritual life, and is the great provider for all graces. Now, to manage this work successfully,

1. Ye must lay all your wants upon him. That moment that Christ and a soul meet in the everlasting covenant, the soul embracing him in the gospel-offer, he says to the soul, as Judg. xix. 20, " Peace be with thee; howsoever, let all thy wants lie upon me." Whatever ye want for soul or body, duty or danger, time or eternity, let it all lie on me. And this is agreeable to the marriage covenant, wherein the provision lies upon the husband, 1 Pet. v. 7. Now faith is to say, " Be it so; from henceforth all my wants be on my Lord." And this implies two things.

(1.) Renouncing of self-provision, or living on one's own stock and purchase; Matth. xvi. 24, " If any man will come after me let him deny himself." Faith empties a soul of itself; it is a man's going out of himself to Jesus Christ for all. While the provision brought from Egypt lasted, the manna fell not; and while men are busy bringing forth of their own store for their needs, the treasure in heaven is locked upon them; but it is opened to the self-emptied believer; Luke i. 53, " He hath filled the hungry with good things, and the rich he hath sent empty away."

(2.) Trusting him for the supply of all your wants, betaking yourselves to him to live wholly by him. Ye must be like a poor man, who can do nothing for himself, being utterly unable to work and win any thing, that casts himself on his rich friend for all he needs, Psal. lv. 22, 1 Pet. v. 7, it is a pithy description of faith which we have; Ruth ii. 12, "The Lord God of Israel, under whose wings thou art come to trust;" for the believer is like a silly chicken unable to preserve itself from the bird of prey, getting in under the wings of the dam for protection.

2. Ye must lay your wants before him, table your complaints, and present your petitions unto him, upon whom all your wants are laid, Matth. xxi. 22. Thus Paul did again and again, and brought forth plentifully out of the treasure, 2 Cor. xii. 8, 9. What God has a mind to give, he will yet have his people to seek. And this imports,

(1.) A free unfolding of your case to him, as to your best friend, able and willing to help, Eph. iii. 12. Faith makes the believer pour out his heart to the Lord, Psalm lxii. 8. Ye must unfold it freely, fully, without reserve; for to do otherwise would argue distrust. Many a time the believer's heart is full of griefs, sorrows and anxieties; but the best ease a pained heart can get, is pouring out itself in the bosom of a God in Christ, Cant. vii. 11.

(2.) A resignation of the matter into the hands of the Lord, Psalm xxxvii. 5. He is infinitely wise, and the care of the household of heaven is devolved upon him by his Father, John v. 22. He is to judge what wants are really fit to be supplied to every one, what measures of supply they must have, at what time the supply is to be communicated, and in what manner. And it is the work of faith to leave all these upon him, and rest satisfied in his wise disposal.

3. Ye must believe the promises relative to the supply of your needs; Matth. xxi. 22, "All things whatsoever ye shall ask in prayer, believing, ye shall receive." God will have his people deal with him in the way of trusting of his word of promise. And the more firm trust we have in his word, the more abundantly do we receive of his fulness. They are the breasts of the divine consolations, and faith sucks the sap of them, by believing them; Psalm xxviii. 7, "The Lord is my strength and my shield, my heart trusted in him, and I am helped."

(1.) Ye must believe them as a sure word, that shall certainly be made out, Psalm cxix. 160. The unbelieving world take the promises but for fair words, which they will not trust to; but do thou take them for sure words, big with mercy and favour, which shall not miscarry, but certainly bring forth at the set time, Psalm xii. 6.

(2.) Ye must believe them with a faith of particular application, not only that they shall be made out to others, but that they shall be made out to you, Mark xi. 24; James i. 6, 7. What canst thou be the better of a salve not applied to thy sore, or of a promise not applied to thy soul? The devils may believe that the promises shall be accomplished, but they cannot believe they shall be accomplished to them. In our national covenant we abjure the Pope's general and doubtsome faith. But alas! the applicatory and appropriating act of faith, whereby one appropriates Christ and his benefits to one's self, is much fallen out of our divinity now-a-days, and is in hazard of being extruded, that it may not enter again. The promises are God's blank bills and bonds; if ye do not by faith fill up your own name in them, what will they avail you?" But fill it up by faith, and come forward with them in your hand, saying with David, Psalm cxix. 49, "Remember the word unto thy servant, upon which thou hast caused me to hope."

4. *Lastly*. Wait and hang on about the Lord's hand confidently, till the supply come, using the means of God's appointment for it, Isa. xl. *ult.*; Psalm xxvii. *ult.* Faith and the use of means do sweetly agree, so that they be means of God's appointment, Psalm xxxvii. 3. And they must not be separated. To use means without dependence on the Lord for the success, is atheism; to pretend to believe, and neglect the means of God's institution, is presumption. But be you in the use of means, and wait on him with confident expectation, that what is good the Lord will give. This is it which in the Old Testament is celebrated under the name of trusting, relying, and staying on the Lord. Trust reposed in a generous man, is a strong tie on him to answer expectation, Gen. xix. 8. And they who trust in the Lord shall never be ashamed.

Thus I have shewn you, how you may bring forth out of God's treasure of favour. O ye Christians who have interest in Christ, let this be your daily work; apply to the treasure. For motives, consider,

1. It is a high privilege that it is open to you, and ye have access to it, and will you not improve it? If ye consider that it is shut on the most part of the world, that it was opened to you by the blood of the Son of God, by the operation of the Spirit of God upon you, bringing you to embrace the everlasting covenant, ye will prize that access, and improve it. Had one ready access allowed them to their prince's favour, would they slight it? No surely.

2. This is the Christian life, by which true believers are distinguished from hypocrites, even the life of faith, Gal. ii. 20. And what is that but the daily travelling betwixt their own emptiness and the fulness that is in Jesus Christ? Whereas the hypocrite lives upon his own stock, a stranger to communion with God, and drawing supplies from him in the way of believing. As ever ye would prove yourselves sincere Christians then, take this way.

3. The want of this is the cause that Christians lead such poor lives as they do; Matth. xiii. *ult,* "He did not many mighty works there, because of their unbelief." Many who have cordially embraced Christ in the gospel-offer, spend their time in complaining of their wants, more than applying to the treasure for supply; more in doubting of their interest in Christ, more than in improving it this way; in disputing their right to the treasure of favour in Christ, more than believing. And hence such,

(1.) Unfruitful lives, little progress in holiness, victory over corruption, usefulness for God in their stations, &c., Col. ii. 6, 7. Little faith will always make little holiness; forasmuch as faith purifies the heart, and is the blessed instrument of the soul's communion with God, by which influences from heaven are brought down, without which the soul must needs be in a withered case.

(2.) Uncomfortable lives. God is "the God of consolation," Rom. xv. 5, and the way to obtain it is in the way of believing, ver. 13. The truth is, it is no wonder the Christian, when he looks to himself, be discouraged, and drive heavily, since often he can see nothing there but weakness, darkness, and deadness; but faith looks to Christ, and sees a fulness in him, "Who of God is made unto us wisdom, righteousness, sanctification, and redemption;" Col. ii. 9, 10.

4. This is a day when Christians have much need to keep up communion with God, and live by faith, Eph. v. 16. It is a day wherein religion is like to die out, and the little of it that is left is in hazard of dwindling away, in principle and practice, into mere morality; it is a day of many temptations and snares, and withdrawing of the Spirit, and wherein judgment seems to be hastening on apace, spiritual and temporal judgments too, for that men have not received the truth in the love thereof, and have walked in darkness while they had the light.

5. *Lastly.* They are most welcome to the Lord, who come with the most holy boldness, and oftenest unto him, for supply out of the treasure; Matth. xv. 28, "O woman, great is thy faith: be it unto thee even as thou wilt." Those honour God most, who are most emptied of themselves, and have most business in heaven, for supply

of their wants. It is a pleasure to have full breasts sucked; and there is a fulness in this treasure of favour lodged in Christ. His fulness is not the fulness of a vessel only to serve itself, but of a fountain to be communicated. O then bring forth daily out of it.

UNBELIEF THE SIN AGAINST CHRIST BY WAY OF EMINENCE, AND THE WRONG DONE TO THE SOUL THEREBY.

Proverbs viii. 36,

But he that sinneth against me, wrongeth his own soul; all they that hate me love death.

The preceding verse gave us the happiness of those who are interested in Christ; this verse gives us the misery of those who reject him. And in it we have two things.

1. A dreadful risk some sinners run; they sin against the wisdom of God, and wrong their own souls. In which consider,

(1.) The dangerous adventure they make: they sin against Christ the Son of God. I told you, that Christ the personal wisdom of God is here meant. I must here inquire what is meant by sinning against him. Christ being true God, every sin men commit is against him, and wrongs their souls too. But it is not every sin that is here meant; it is some sin by way of eminency against the second person of the Trinity; for it is such a one as is constructed to be a hating of him, and loving death, which cannot be said of every sin. You know that the Holy Ghost being true God also every sin is in some sort against him; yet there is a sin against the Holy Ghost so called by way of eminency; so here is a sin against Christ by way of eminency. Now those sins which have their denominations from the several persons of the Trinity, respect them not so much in their essence, as in their office, operation, and work. The Father is Creator, the original lawgiver, the Son Redeemer and Saviour, the Holy Ghost applier of Christ's purchase, Enlightener and Sanctifier. The first sin of Adam in him and us, and the sins of the Pagans still, are the sin against the Father, the transgressing of the law of the Creator. The sin of gospel-despisers is the sin against the Son, as a rejecting of the gospel of Christ. The sin of obstinate and malicious deliberate fighting against God, is the sin against the Holy Ghost, as against the inward working of the Holy Ghost in them. All the world are by nature under the first, and so liable to wrath; but the Son of God is the anointed Saviour and Redeemer, by whom alone sinners may be recovered. John xiv. 6. He is the ordinance of God for sinners' salvation. He is the remedy against sin provided by the Father; so the rejecting of this ordinance and remedy is the sin against Christ. That is, in a word, it is the sin opposite to the seeking and finding of Christ, vers. 34, 35, namely, not closing with, but rejecting Christ offered in the Gospel, called the sin of unbelief, John xvi. 8, 9.

(2.) The effect of this dangerous adventure; he wrongeth his own soul. The word properly imports violence, and might be read, "He doth violence to his own soul." So it is rendered, Zeph. iii. 4. He ruins himself, he is a self-destroyer, a self-murderer. The man is lying pining away in his sin; Christ the Physician comes to his bedside, saying, "Sinner, I offer you life and salvation with myself." But he turns away, he will have none of him, he cannot part with his disease. So he wrongs his own soul; he dies of it. But there is more than that in it. The man slights Christ; who loses by it? Not Christ, not his messengers, but the poor unbeliever himself. Prov. ix. 12.

2. The nature of this practice, which shews what a dreadful risk it must needs be. But of that more afterwards.

Two doctrines may be deduced from the words.

DOCTRINE I. Unbelief, or a sinner's not believing, accepting, embracing, closing with, and resting on Christ for salvation, is the sin against Christ by way of eminency.

DOCT. II. The unbeliever sinning against Christ by unbelief, wrongs his own soul.

I shall illustrate each doctrine in order.

DOCT. I. Unbelief, or a sinner's not believing, accepting, embracing, closing with, and resting on Christ for salvation, is the sin against Christ by way of eminency. That is, if a man designed an affront to the Son of God, if he were in a mind to pierce him to the heart, and put a signal affront on him, this is the way to do it, namely, to slight the offer he makes of himself in the gospel.

In handling this doctrine, I shall,

I. Shew what treatment of Christ it is, that is this sinning against him.

II. Confirm the doctrine, shewing you, that unbelief is the sin against Christ; that this treatment of Christ, in not believing in, accepting, embracing, closing with, and resting on him for salvation, is sinning against him in an eminent manner.

III. Improve the subject, in an address both to saints and sinners.

I. I am to shew what treatment of Christ it is, that is this sinning against him. In the general, it is twofold.

First, There is a doctrinal treatment of him, that is this sinning against him. So Deists, Socinians, Arians, Papists, &c., sin against him. I insist not on this further than to warn you, that there is, at this day, in this island, appearing a greater disposition to depart from the faith, than there has been at least these thirty years past. Some in the neighbouring land, not papists, nor prelatists, but dissenters, are undermining the doctrine of the eternal Godhead of Christ; and some in this Church are making woful advances towards obscuring the doctrine of the free grace of God in Christ. All which are the native bitter fruits of the generation's practical slighting of, and sinning against Christ, under the light of the gospel.

Secondly, There is a practical treatment of him, that is this sinning against him. And of this kind is,

1. Living ignorant of Christ, and the fundamental truths of the gospel; John i. 10. Grossly ignorant persons are doubtless unbelievers. For how can they believe, who know not what to believe? how can they believe in Christ, who have no knowledge of him? Psalm ix. 10. They are slighters of Christ, who have means of knowledge, and yet know him not; they know him not, because they will not be acquainted with him; Job xxi. 14, "They say unto God, Depart from us; for we desire not the knowledge of thy ways." And thus many proclaim their soul-ruining unbelief, by their slighting of ordinances and means of knowledge, and not profiting under them. Were there a physician in the country-side curing all freely, and if any should never use means to get acquainted with him, would not such persons be slighters of him, to their own ruin.

2. People's living insensible of their absolute need of Christ; Matth. ix. 12. He comes in the gospel, and offers himself with all his salvation to sinners, to every one that hears it. Why does he so, but because they must perish without him, and that they need him? But the most part find no pinching need of him, and therefore never come to him. This is slighting him with a witness; Rev. iii. 17, "Because thou sayest, I am rich, and increased with goods, and have need of nothing; and knowest not that thou art wretched, and miserable, and poor, and blind, and naked." The law is preached, and their misery without Christ is told them; yet are they never so far convinced as to be pricked to the heart; Acts ii. 37. They have no more ado with him, than a hale and sound person with the physician.

3. Their not believing the doctrine of the gospel, the record that God hath given concerning his Son; 1 John v. 10, 11. In the gospel it is testified to us from heaven, That Christ alone is the great ordinance of God for life and salvation to poor sinners; that God hath placed that life in him, and offers it in and with him to them. This is the doctrine of the gospel; but who believes it? Is. liii. 1. OBJECT. Who does not believe it? ANSW. Alas; that is the nature of the disease. Men may convince men who are hearers of the gospel of the sin of murder, adultery, &c.; but if the Spirit of God take it not in hand, they will not convince them of unbelief; John xvi. 8, 9. But for your conviction, (which may the Spirit carry home!) I will tell you, the treatment which Christ gets from most men, upon the back of the revelation of that record that God hath given of him to them, is such as that; 1 Sam. x. 24, 27, "And Samuel said to all the people, See ye him whom the Lord hath chosen, that there is none like him among all the people?—But the children of Belial said, How shall this man save us? and they despised him;" and as that, 2 Kings v. 10—12, "And Elisha sent a messenger unto him, saying, Go and wash in Jordan seven times, and thy flesh shall come again unto thee, and thou shalt be clean. But Naaman was wroth, and went away, and said, Behold, I thought, he will surely come out to me, and stand, and call on the name of the Lord his God, and strike his hand over the place, and recover the leper. Are not Abana, and Pharpar, rivers of Damascus, better than all the waters of Israel? may I not wash in them and be clean! So he turned, and went away in a rage." Of this treatment of Christ take these two evidences.

EVID. 1. Their not seeking after him with the utmost diligence, till they find him. Compare Prov. viii. 34, 36, "Blessed is the man that heareth me, watching daily at my gates, waiting at the posts of my doors.—But he that sinneth against me, wrongeth his own soul; all they that hate me, love death." Paul believed the excellency of the knowledge of Christ Jesus, and therefore pressed forward, Phil. iii. 14. If you were desperately wounded, and one told you of an infallible cure that one had, and which you might get; if after this notice given you, you did not with your utmost might and most laborious endeavours seek after it, would not all the world conclude you did not believe there was such a remedy to be got by you? But your souls are thus wounded, and we tell you day by day, that there is an infallible remedy for them in Christ; and yet ye do not diligently seek after him till ye find him. May we not then say, with the prophet, "Who hath believed our report?" Isa. liii. 1.

Evid. 2. Their seeking life and salvation another way. So do all unbelievers, who give not up themselves to utter despair. They leave the King's highway, John xiv. 6, and betake themselves every one to his own way, Isa. liii. 6. God says of Christ, "This is the way, walk ye in it." But they will not venture on it, but take another way, by which they turn their backs on Christ, and so sin against him.

(1.) The way of the law or covenant of works, namely, by doing to seek life, Rom. ix. 32. This is the way that all men naturally betake themselves to, and that every man abides in, till the grace of God bring him to Jesus Christ. The natural bias of the heart to it I have shewn elsewhere, together with the enmity of the heart against Jesus Christ.* It is little they do; but it is according to their doing, not according to their interest in the blood of Christ, that they expect to find favour with God. This speaks unbelief, and slighting of Christ with a witness; "for if righteousness come by the law, then Christ is dead in vain," Gal. ii. *ult.*

(2.) The way of uncovenanted mercy. They pretend to do what they can; and where they come short, they expect that God will be merciful to them and forgive them; while in the meantime they do not consider that they can only find mercy being in Christ. Thus they do at least mix their own righteousness with Christ's, if they have any regard to Christ at all, Gal. iii. 12.

4. Their not believing the doctrine of the gospel upon the authority of a divine testimony, but on some low account. As to many pretending to believe in Christ, we may see the quite contrary in them to that, 1 Thess. ii. 13,—"When ye received the word of God which ye heard of us, ye received it not as the word of men, but (as it is in truth) the word of God." What belief they have of it, they owe to their education, not to regeneration; to the teaching of men, not to the teaching of the Spirit. What makes some Jews, Mahometans, Pagans, Papists, in foreign countries, namely, that it is the religion they were brought up in, that is even the thing which makes them Christians in our country. O Sirs, that is not faith in Christ, but real unbelief of him, and slighting of him, as receiving his doctrine not upon his own authority, and the testimony of the Spirit, but of man, John v. 34. If ever ye come to honour Christ by believing, your faith will be built on another foundation; John iv. 42, "Now we believe, not because of thy saying: for we have heard him ourselves, and know that this is indeed the Christ, the Saviour of the world."

* See "Fourfold State," state 2, head 1, under the title, "Of the corruption of man's nature."

5. Their not believing the doctrine of the gospel with a particular application to their own case, or to themselves. Here is the trial of a convinced sinner. Christ said, Mark xvi. 15, 16, "Go ye into all the world, and preach the gospel to every creature." "He that believeth and is baptized, shall be saved; but he that believeth not, shall be damned." Hereupon the apostle says to the jailor at Philippi, "Believe in the Lord Jesus Christ, and thou shalt be saved, and thy house," Acts xvi. 31. And every minister of Christ may say so to every man, and God says it to every one to whom his word comes. So that although we do believe that Christ is able and willing to save all his elect, yet if I do not believe that he is able and willing to save ME, and that he offers himself to ME, I am still an unbeliever, and do sin against Christ. For,

(1.) The offer is general, and comprehends us all, Isa. lv. 1; Rev. iii. 20. If any of you then believe it as to all others, and not as to yourselves, ye make God a liar, and do not believe his word; because though God says, the offer is to all that hear the gospel, ye contradict it, saying, that the offer belongs not to you, and that Christ is not willing to be yours.

(2.) What benefit can any man have by a general promise or offer of mercy from God or man, which he does not appropriate to himself? A king offers mercy to all the rebels that will take it; one says, "O but it is to all the rest, and not to me, I will not venture out of my lurking-hole." Is not this a belying of the king, and a refusing of mercy, and slighting the offer?

(3.) How is it possible that one can accept, receive, and rest on Christ for salvation, if he make not a particular application of the promise of the gospel, or gospel-offer to himself? The acceptance, &c. must needs be founded on the offer, and can be no larger than the offer is; if I do not believe that God offers to be my God in Christ, I cannot accept him as such. If I do not believe that Christ gives himself to ME in the gospel-offer, I cannot accept, receive, and embrace, nor rest on him.

(4.) Wherein does our faith of the promises of the gospel go beyond the faith of devils, if it proceed not the length of application of them to ourselves? James ii. 19. The devils believe the threatenings of God, and that with application, and they tremble; and that they believe the promises of God too in the general, that they shall be made out, we have no reason to doubt, when we consider, they believe God's faithfulness to his word, and therefore tremble in expectation of what he has threatened. And they know it is the same faithful God who has made the promises, that has made the threatenings. And now that for a course of five thousand years they have observed the promises still fulfilled in their time, we may be sure that they do expect the rest will be fulfilled too. Wherein then can our faith go beyond theirs, if we believe not the promise or offer of life and salvation to us in particular?

Wherefore in not believing, accepting, embracing, closing with, and resting on Christ for salvation, with particular application to ourselves, we sin against Christ, and wrong our own souls. Against this Satan bends his force, and under a vail of humility Christ is affronted by the unbelieving sinner; and indeed it is a mighty thing to believe this, over the belly of seen and felt vileness and unworthiness; but faith will make its way over it all, and honour Christ by believing his word.

6. *Lastly*. Their not taking, accepting, and receiving of Christ in the Gospel-offer, and resting on him, for life and salvation; John i. 11, 12. The royal Bridgroom is slighted, sinned against, and affronted when the offered marriage is neglected, refused, or shifted, or in any ways not concluded, by the sinful children of Adam; when the bride halts betwixt two opinions, and does not conclude the blessed bargain. And thus sinners sin against Christ,

1st, When the sinner will not take Christ, but holds by other lovers, namely, the world and lusts. There are two opposite parties in suit of sinners' hearts, who are hearers of the gospel, Christ on the one hand, lusts on the other. These last have so engaged the hearts of many, that they give Christ the refusal; Jer. li. 25; John v. 40. They see there is no dealing with both; if they take Christ, they must let these go away; and therefore since they cannot otherwise have him, they will not have him. They cannot think of being deprived or abridged of their sinful liberty; so the offer of Christ is made them, but they will not accept it.

2dly, When the sinner dare not take Christ, or embrace him in the gospel-offer, fearing that he will never be his, nor give himself to him. This is the snare for the convinced sinner, and as effectually keeps him from Christ, as the love of lusts does the secure; Jer. ii. 25. One may see, that the former makes way for the latter. The ground of this is one's sinfulness and unworthiness seen and felt, which makes them think it would be presumption in them to believe. Hence they say, as Luke v. 8. "Depart from me, for I am a sinful man, O Lord." The hand of Joab is in this. Satan has two glasses to let men see their sins in.

(1.) A lessening glass, which he holds before the eyes of secure sinners, causing their sins appear little. Hence their enormous outbreakings, though habitual, are accounted but infirmities; and lesser sins, which the world makes no bones of, are accounted no sins at all.

(2.) A magnifying glass, which he holds before the eyes of the convinced sinner. And one may know that he is looking on his sinful self in Satan's glass, when he sees his own sinfulness so as he cannot see God's mercy, the virtue of Christ's blood, and the efficacy of his Spirit, above his sinfulness; when the sight of the disease sets him farther from the Physician, and makes him stand off from Christ, instead of running to him; when instead of quickening him to embrace the remedy, it causes his heart to faint so as he cannot put forth his hand to apply the offered cure.

That this is from Satan, is manifest, in that it is directly contrary, (1.) To the true use of the law in subserviency to the gospel; Gal. iii. 24. The law discovers sin, and the soul's misery by it; but then the design of that to the hearers of the gospel is, that they may be made to prize and run unto Christ. (2.) To the ample declarations of love and mercy made in the gospel, which shew that there is no case whatsoever so bad but Christ is both able and willing to take it in hand; Isa. i. 18, and lv. 1; Rev. iii. 20, and xxii. 17.

3*dly*, When the sinner dare not venture on Christ alone for salvation, but to strengthen that bottom, goes about to render himself acceptable to God by his own obedience, Gal. v. 4. The covenant of works is so engrained in our natures, and so ignorant are we naturally of the mystery of Christ, and the way of imputed righteousness; that till the Spirit of the Lord savingly enlighten one in the knowledge of Christ, he will have but low thoughts of an imputed righteousness as an insecure way, and will therefore go about to strengthen it by the addition of his own works; though it is but attempting to mix clay with iron, that will not do. But the Spirit of the Lord, in the day of power, will carry men quite off their own bottom.

4*thly*, When the sinner does not take him for all the ends for which he is appointed of the Father for sinners, and in all his offices, but divides them, 1 Cor. i. 30. He is given to us for all in the gospel-offer, for salvation from sin as well as from wrath, to be our Prophet to teach us, our Priest to save us, and our King to govern us. When therefore the sinner does not take him for sanctification as well as justification, he is not received at all indeed, but sinned against, and rejected as the ordinance for sanctifying of sinners.

Lastly, When the sinner does not believe, that he shall have life and salvation by Jesus Christ. True faith may be accompanied with many doubtings; sometimes one may be ready to say, "My hope is perished from the Lord;" but it is plain that where there is no such persuasion in greater or lesser measure at any time, there is no faith.

II. I proceed to confirm the doctrine, shewing you, that unbelief is the sin against Christ; that this treatment of Christ, in not believing in, accepting, embracing, closing with, and resting on Christ for salvation, is sinning against him in an eminent manner. This will appear from some general considerations, and from a view of some particular pieces of malignity against Christ wrapt up in unbelief.

First, It appears from some general considerations.

1. Faith in Christ is an honouring of him in a special manner, John v. 23, 24; therefore unbelief must be a special dishonour done to him. Faith gives glory to the object of it, Rom. iv. 20; unbelief then robs him of that glory, and casts reproach on him. Faith puts the crown on Christ's head, Cant. iii. *ult.*, unbelief pulls it off and tramples it under foot. See then how good, necessary, and pleasing to Christ believing in him is; how bad, noxious, and abominable to him unbelief must be.

2. Unbelief is the great Antichrist in the heart, setting up there in downright opposition to the Son of God. The end of Christ's coming was to destroy sin, 1 John iii. 8, the effect of unbelief is to preserve sin in life and vigour. It is the soul and life of all other sins, the shield that keeps their heads and hearts hale; take it away, they all die, and the soul revives; leave it upon their head, and they all live, and the soul dies, John viii. 24. It is the general of the army of hell in men's breasts, against whom the word is given in the day of power, " Fight neither with small nor great," but with unbelief, the king of sins, John xvi. 8, 9.

3. It is a sin that so engrosses the whole soul to itself against Christ, that it leaves him nothing to take part with him against it. If a man sin against Christ by oppression, murder, &c. his judgment, reason, natural conscience, will in greater or lesser measure plead the Lord's cause against him, and will prepare the way for the Spirit's conviction. But as for unbelief, there is no help from them against it. The mystery of Christ lies beyond the ken of mere reason, 1 Cor. ii. 14, how then can the blackness of the sin of unbelief be discerned thereby, or the natural conscience check for it? Nay, mere reason, in its corrupt state, sides against Christ with unbelief, in as far as the best way it knows, is the way of the law or covenant of works. So that on this occasion, Meroz's curse may light on all the faculties of the soul, " because they come not to the help of the Lord against the mighty," Judg. v. 23.

4. It is the sin that ruins the hearers of the gospel, with whom Christ has to do; John iii. 18, 19, ",He that believeth not, is condemned already, because he hath not believed in the name of the

only begotten Son of God. And this is the condemnation, that light is come into the world, and men loved darkness rather than light, because their deeds were evil." The poor pagans who have not heard of Christ, sin not against him in this sort, John xv. 22. Whatever sins the hearers of the gospel may have been chargeable with, if they will believe in Christ, they shall never be charged on them; upon this point of believing, or not believing, turns their salvation, or damnation, Mark xvi. 16. Wherefore since it is the ruining sin, it must needs be the great ruining sin against Christ.

5. It is equal to the grossest sins against the light of nature. The Pharisee could say, I am not unjust, an extortioner, an adulterer; the publican durst not say so. But the one rejected the propitiation, which the other embraced, Luke xviii. 13, and so was accepted of God, while the other was rejected. You will bless God ye are honest, sober men and women, no adulterers, murderers, &c.; but ye do not see the bloody sin of unbelief, which is as ill as any of them; Isa. lxvi. 3, "He that killeth an ox, is as if he slew a man;" i.e. An unbeliever is as a murderer in God's sight. Faith was the great duty under the Old Testament as well as under the New, ver. 2. And those Jews who put their sacrifices of oxen, lambs, and their incense, in the Messiah's stead, by unbelief were as murderers, &c.

6. It is above these sins in odiousness and heinousness; Heb. x. 28, 29, "He that despised Moses' law, died without mercy, under two or three witnesses: of how much sorer punishment, suppose ye shall he be thought worthy, who hath trodden under foot the Son of God," &c.? There was a consultation of the Trinity concerning the making of man, and the result was, his creation after God's image. How great must those sins be, which, breaking the laws of his creation, do signally deface that image? There was also a consultation of the Trinity concerning man's restoration, and the result was, the Son of God giving himself to the death for their recovery. How much greater then must the sin of unbelief be, which of its own nature tends to make the whole contrivance vain? The Sodomites were great sinners, and the Capernaumites unbelievers; which were the greatest sinners? The greatest punishment by a just Judge speaks the greatest sin; and so the Capernaumite unbelievers were the greatest sinners, Matth. xi. 23, 24.

7. It has none that goes beyond it but the sin against the Holy Ghost; and even it is unbelief carried to its utmost height, Heb. x. 29. Unbelief strikes against the Father and the Son, casting dishonour on both, John v. 23. If to this be added a doing despite to the Spirit of God, the sinner is at his utmost pitch of wickedness. And none are capable of the latter, but he that is guilty of the former.

8. *Lastly*, It is a sin directly striking against the glorious office wherewith Christ is invested, and while he is in the actual exercise of that office, John viii. 49. The Father minding to recover the glory of his wronged attributes, and lost sinners of the race of Adam, invested his own Son in the mediatory office, that he should build the temple of the Lord, and bear the glory. The Son comes in this his noble office, with his Father's commission, to prosecute it for these noble ends: and unbelief rejects him as such, and casts dishonour on him, Luke xix. 14. To do a personal injury to a king is a crime, but to do an injury striking against his kingly character and office, and that while he is in the administration of his royal office, is a crime of a far deeper die, than any merely personal injury done him. So the case is here.

Secondly, That unbelief is the sin against Christ by way of eminency, appears from a view of some particular pieces of malignity against him wrapt up therein.

1. It is a despising him as the Father's choice. The voice of the gospel is, "This is my beloved Son, in whom I am well pleased," Matth. iii. *ult.* The unbeliever answers, "We will not have this man to reign over us," Luke xix. 14. When man fell, God looked on the whole creation, and there was none found able to help him; so he made choice of his own Son, that the breach might be under his hand, Psalm lxxxix. 19. This comes to be proclaimed in the gospel, and as Samuel said to all the people, "See ye him whom the Lord hath chosen, that there is none like him among all the people?" 1 Sam. x. 24; it says, "Behold my servant whom I uphold, mine elect in whom my soul delighteth," Isa. xlii. 1. "Behold the Lamb of God, which taketh away the sin of the world," John i. 29. But unbelief says, as 1 Sam. x. 27, "How shall this man save us? and they despise him." So unbelievers pour contempt on the choice. Ask the unbelieving Jews if they approve the choice? No; they say, It is a stumbling-block; ask the unbelieving Gentiles, if they approve it, No, it is foolishness, 1 Cor. i. 23. Therefore do others as they will, they will not lay their weight on that bottom. Only believers cry, Grace, grace to the choice! a noble choice! "Christ the wisdom of God, and the power of God," ver. 24; compare Matth. xi. 6.

2. It is a trampling upon his love in undertaking the mediatory office. Man having sinned, justice demands satisfaction; the poor bankrupts cannot discharge the debt themselves, angels found themselves too weak to bear such a burden, sacrifice and offering cannot be accepted as a compensation for the wrong done to a holy God. The proposal is made to the Son, and respect to his Father's glory, and unhired love to sinners, makes him accept and strike hands; "Lo, I come," &c., Psalm xl. 6, 7. And after all, unbelief says in

effect, he might have let it alone; the unbeliever is not for life and salvation that way. Christ's Father is content, he is so, but the unbeliever is not, Psalm lxxxi. 11. How great must the sin of trampling on such love be?

3. It is a treating of him as a liar and an impostor. The language of every unbeliver is that; John vii. 12, "He deceiveth the people." Christ's name is the word of God, by whom the mind of God touching the salvation of sinners is manifested to the world; he is by office interpreter of the Father's mind, the great prophet and teacher. He came from the Father's bosom, and reveals the way of salvation in the doctrine of the gospel. What is it not to believe him then, but to make him a liar? 1 John v. 10. And since the revelation made by him is upon such a weighty matter, the not believing it must needs infer the looking on him as an impostor. What then shall be given to that false heart, that thus sins against Christ? "Sharp arrows of the mighty, with coals of juniper," Psalm cxx. 4.

4. It is a contempt poured on his precious blood, and the whole course of his obedience and sufferings. The believer by faith gets in under that blood, Heb. xii. 24; but unbelief treads on it, chap. x. 29. This performance of the Son was looked upon as a sufficient mean to retrieve the Father's glory, and recover the sinner that was sunk lowest in sin and misery, Psalm lxxxix. 19. As such it is proposed to sinners in the gospel; but they will not receive it. And if ye consider all the sets of unbelievers, the bold contemners that go on in their sins, and hope for mercy; the legal professors that lay the stress on their own duties; the trembling unbeliever, that dare not come to Christ; the desperate sinner, that says there is no hope; they will all be found agreeing in maintaining low unworthy thoughts of the glorious ransom paid by Christ, and offered to them. The first say, All that was needless, God is merciful; the second, It is too weak a bottom to trust all to; the third, It may bear the weight of many, but it is too weak for theirs; the fourth, It can do nothing for them.

5. It is a frustrating of the ends of the death of Christ, as far as lies in the unbeliever's power. He had a long, sore, and helpless travail of soul; he endured it in hopes of a glorious issue; Isa. liii. 11; Heb. xii. 2. But did all treat him as the unbelieving part of the world does, the issue would be but as it were bringing forth wind. At the expense of the blood of the Son of God, a medicine is prepared for perishing souls; but the unbeliever will not apply it, when it is brought to his hand; a feast is prepared, but the unbeliever will not eat of it, but says in effect, "To what purpose is this waste?"

6. *Lastly.* It is a declining of his government, and subjection to him, most reproachfully; Luke xix. 14. We see most of the hearers of the gospel at this pass with him; subject themselves to whom they will, they will not subject themselves to him; they stick by other lords. His Father has given him all power in heaven and earth; but they will not come under his power, as long as they can shift otherwise. There are many reasons of this, but there is one that is little observed, namely, unbelief, they cannot trust him. A wise people will not subject themselves willingly to one they cannot trust; Judg. ix. 15, compare Psalm ii. *ult.* They cannot trust him with their welfare, though he is the Father's trustee, the trustee of believers; hence they say, he shall not be their trustee. What wonder then that unbelief be a "piercing of him?" Zech. xii. 10.

From this doctrine we may learn lessons for saints, for sinners, and for all.

First, Here is a lesson for saints, or believers.

1. Prize the precious faith which God has given you 2 Pet. i. 1. Have your souls been brought to believe in, accept, and embrace Jesus Christ offered in the gospel, for all his salvation, and so to come off from the course of slighting and sinning against Christ. Do not undervalue it as a small thing, but look to the nature of reigning unbelief, and prize it next to the gift of his precious Son and Spirit. If it were but as a grain of mustard-seed, it is more precious than all the gold of the Indies, more precious than as many faithless works and duties, as would have filled up every minute of your time since ye were born.

2. Wonder at his sparing you till ye were brought the length of believing in him. How deep did your unbelief go against him; what attribute of his did it not cast dirt upon; what was it he did or suffered, but it had an ill tale of? O, why did he put up all these affronts, and still insist on your believing, giving you his word, writ, seal, oath, and whatsoever could have been required of the most faithless man, to cause you believe him, till ye were won to faith in him?

3. Mourn over your remaining unbelief, as the father of the child did, Mark ix. 25, who said with tears, "Lord I believe! help thou mine unbelief." Jealousies of Christ are a disease that runs in the veins of all those of the blood royal of heaven, ay till they get home to their Father's house. How justly may he say, "O faithless generation! how long shall I be with you? how long shall I suffer you." Alas! can the saints' experiences of his truth and faithfulness, and the tried word, carry them no further? If there could be any such uneasy passion as shame in heaven, they would blush for their unbelief whenever they got in there.

4. *Lastly*, See what it is that mars the communication betwixt Christ and you, and what makes you lead such a poor life, both in point of sanctification and comfort, Matth. xiii. *ult.*, "He did not many mighty works there, because of their unbelief." Faith purifies the heart, unbelief makes it as the neglected garden, overgrown with weeds. Faith quiets the heart and cheers it, Rom. xv. 13. David's experience of the way of getting help from heaven we have, Psalm xxviii. 7, "My heart trusted in him, and I am helped." Trust reposed in a generous man, able to help, brings him to put to his hand speedily, for the help of the party trusting him. No wonder that unbelief, being of such a nature, mar the communication.

Secondly, Here is a lesson for sinners, or unbelievers.

1. Ye are sinners against Christ in an eminent manner. Our text brings you in guilty of affronting the Son of God, sinning against the remedy of sin. Though the language of your lips may be "Hosanna to the Son of David;" the language of your unbelieving hearts is, Crucify him. Ye are guilty of sinning against him at the rate which Pagans, yea and devils, never sinned against him. They broke the law of their Creator; but ye have not only done so, but ye are breaking the law of redeeming love, namely, the law of faith, too.

2. Here is a sin thou hast to be sensible of, and mourn for, which hitherto thou hast little regarded. May be thou hast sometimes been grieved for other sins, and mourned for them. But didst thou ever mourn for this? did ever this give thee a grieved heart? Truly this is the wound to the heart, this is the most dangerous evil, that keeps all the rest from healing. If ye have not been sensible of and affected with it, (1.) Your faith is likely to be but a fancy, the Spirit being promised for that end, John xvi. 8, 9. (2.) Your unbelief would be sure to be strengthened by all your other mourning for sin; and so instead of its bringing you nearer Christ, it would set you farther off from him, Matth. xxi. 31.

3. Here, even here, O sinner, lies your ruin for time and eternity, John viii. 24, "If ye believe not that I am he, ye shall die in your sins." Mark xvi. 16, "He that believeth not shall be damned." This is the great soul-murdering sin among gospel-hearers, for it is the sinning against the remedy of sin. Consider, (1.) It makes all your other plague-sores incurable, while it is not removed, John viii. 24. Your pride, passion, worldliness, &c. still run upon you; why, so they will always do, while the bloody issue of unbelief is not stopped. While that remains, they can admit no cure but a palliative one, after which they must needs break out again. For the falling dew shall as soon make its way through the flinty rock, as sanctifying influences shall come into you without union with Christ, which is

marred by unbelief. (2.) At this rate then ye must die in your sins eternally, and your unbelief must be the great cause of your ruin, 2. Thess. i. 8.

4. The condemnation of unbelievers must be most dreadful, since it is the sin against Christ, Matth. xi. 24, "It shall be more tolerable for the land of Sodom in the day of judgment than for thee." Other sins wound the soul; this resolutely keeps the wounds open, and will not suffer them to be healed. Other sins are against the sovereign authority of God in the law; this superadds thereto a contempt of unparalleled love and mercy opened to the sinner in the gospel. As then the sourest vinegar comes off the most generous wine, so the most fearful thunder-claps of wrath will break out on the sinner, from the contempt of a throne of grace through unbelief.

5. *Lastly*, Here is what may strike the bottom out of all your objections against your believing in Christ, fetch them from what quarter ye will, and dress them up in what form you please, whether the conclusion be, you may not, dare not, or ought not believe on Christ. As it is the commandment "That we should believe on the name of his Son Jesus Christ," 1 John iii. 23, so not believing is the sin against Christ. Account ye of it as ye will, he will reckon it the greatest affront that ye can do him, and he will reckon with you for it as such. Wherefore let this short answer serve in the case.

Thirdly, Here is a lesson for all. It concerns us all to be convinced of the malignity against Christ and his Father that is in the sin of unbelief, to get above it, as we would throw coals of hell-fire out of our bosom; to believe in Christ, embrace him as our Saviour and Redeemer, Head and Husband, and to live by faith on him. This is the way to honour the Son, the true way to be holy here, and happy hereafter.

DOCTRINE II. The unbeliever sinner against Christ by unbelief, wrongs his own soul.

Here I shall shew, how the unbeliever sinning against Christ by unbelief, wrongs his own soul; and then deduce an inference or two for application.

I. I am to shew how the unbeliever, sinning against Christ by unbelief, wrongs his own soul. The wrong here meant is real hurt or damage, arising from this woful practice. Now, on whom does it fall? On the sinner himself. I take it up in these two, that he wrongs his own soul really and only.

First, The unbeliever, sinning against Christ by unbelief, wrongs his own soul really. He does in very deed do hurt and bring damage to himself, not to his body only, but to his soul, the more precious part. He does violence to himself, he treats his own soul cruelly and unjustly. He carries against his own soul as an enemy, doing it real mischief. For by unbelief,

1*st*, A man keeps his soul in a state of separation and alienation from God. The sinner by nature is far from God, without God in the world, Eph. ii. 12. Jesus Christ is the only way to the Father, John xiv. 6, and unbelief keeps the soul from off that way, fixes the separation wall, that as long as it remains in its power, the sinner can never meet with God, as rejecting the only meeting place.

2*dly*, A man keeps his soul under the guilt of all his sins. The blood of Jesus purgeth from all sin; but it must be sprinkled by faith on the soul, which unbelief refuseth, John viii. 24. It keeps the soul out of Christ; and while it is so, all the guilt remains, the yoke of his transgressions is wreathed about his neck, and all the cords of death abide about him in their force. No mourning or sorrow, tears or repentance will loose them; only the blood of Christ procures pardon.

3*dly*, A man keeps his soul in a state of utter inability to do any thing that is good or acceptable in the sight of God; Heb. xi. 6, "Without faith it is impossible to please him." It keeps the reigning power of sin hale in the soul, and so preserves and feeds the several lusts, the devourers of the soul. It binds up hand and foot that he can do nothing, nor move a step heavenward, John xv. 5. For it blocks up all saving communication between heaven and the soul.

4*thly*, It fixes the soul in a state of condemnation; John iii. 18, "He that believeth not is condemned already." It keeps it under the curse of the first covenant, and exposes it to eternal destruction. It keeps it naked without a righteousness, destitute of any valid plea for eternal life. It leaves it without the city of refuge, every moment in hazard of being cut off by the avenger of blood.

Lastly, By refusing the remedy, the unbeliever brings double ruin on his own soul. The soul might be saved; but by unbelief salvation is refused, and so the soul is in worse case than if Christ had never been offered to it.

Secondly, The unbeliever sinning against Christ by unbelief, wrongs his own soul only, not Christ whom he sins against; Prov. ix. 12, "If thou be wise, thou shalt be wise for thyself; but if thou scornest, thou alone shalt bear it." All sin is against the mind and honour of Christ, but no sin is against his happiness. If all the creatures did conspire against him, it could not make the least diminution of his happiness, or in the least disturb him. Thy unbelief is like one's rushing his head against a rock, which can only hurt the person himself; Job xxxv. 6, "If thou sinnest, what dost thou against him? or if thy transgressions be multiplied, what dost thou unto him?"

I shall conclude this subject with some inferences.

1. All unbelievers, rejecters of Christ, are self-murderers; they ruin their own souls, Ezek. xviii. 31. When it comes to pass that thy soul perishes, and inquiry is made, by whose hands it has fallen, there will be a decision; Hos. xiii. 9, "O Israel, thou hast destroyed thyself;" not Adam, not Satan, but thou thyself, O sinner.

2. Ye cannot do your souls a worse turn than not to receive Christ by faith. Many an ill turn ye have done them by swearing, lying, covetousness, &c., but this is a stab to the heart; this is wounding the soul in the most sensible, in the most noble part.

3. All unbelievers will be inexcusable. Pagans will have something to say, that the revelation of the way of salvation through Christ was not made to them; yea devils will have it to say, that there was no remedy prepared for them. But what wilt thou have to say for thyself, O unbeliever, who treadest under foot the blood of the Redeemer! Thou wilt be wholly without excuse. Thou wilt be like the man that sat down at the table, at the marriage of the king's son, without a wedding-garment, who when asked, how he came there not having a wedding-garment, was speechless, having no excuse to allege for his presumptuous behaviour.

4. Believe in, accept of, embrace, and close with Christ, as ye would not ruin your own souls. Refuse not the remedy that is freely provided for you in Christ. Ye are all invited and welcome to come unto Christ for salvation from sin, and from the wrath that is to come. By accepting of Christ ye shall be saved, and your souls shall have communion with God. But if ye believe not, you shall perish, and the wrath of God shall lie on you for ever. "He that believeth, shall be saved; but he that believeth not, shall be damned," Mark xvi. 16.

5. *Lastly*, Saints and believers, in as far as ye admit unbelief, ye wrong your own souls. Every act of unbelief is a doing violence to your souls, and hurting them in their most essential interests. O then guard against this dreadful and deceitful enemy, that seeks your ruin. Daily exercise faith in Christ, improve it by vigorous and repeated exercise; and continually cry unto the Lord, saying, "Lord increase our faith." Live by faith, walk by faith, and, in the strength of Christ, resist all the assaults of unbelief; and in due time ye shall be more than conquerors through him that loved you. Always bear in mind, and never forget, that "he that sinneth

against Christ, wrongeth his own soul," and is in love with death; whereas he that honoureth him by believing in his name, and is strong in the faith, giving glory to God, shall be safe amidst all the troubles and trials of this world, in every period and stage of life, and shall at last be received into the house not made with hands, eternal in the heavens, where happiness for ever dwells, and the voice of violence and wrong is never heard.

BELIEVERS A MYSTERY, WITH A DESCRIPTION OF THEIR TRAVELS FROM THE WILDERNESS OF THIS WORLD, TO THE HEAVENLY CANAAN, LEANING UPON CHRIST.*

Song viii. 5,

Who is this that cometh up from the wilderness, leaning upon her Beloved?

WE have been solemnising our souls' espousals to Jesus Christ, and our consent to the gospel-call, saying in effect to us, "Wilt thou go with this man?" Leave thy father's house, and thine own people, and cleave to the King of Zion. We have before angels and men answered, We will go with him, for he is our Beloved. Here we have an account of the Christian life, which must be our life, if we will deal honestly with him; it is a "coming up out of the wilderness, leaning on our Beloved." These are the words of the daughters of Jerusalem, containing,

1. An inquiry about a party, whom they took particular notice of, namely, the church of believers, the spouse of Christ; "Who is this?" It intimates a kind of surprise, Who's that! The wilderness uses not to afford such a sight as this. It imports an admiration as of some hidden thing, a mystery; Who is this? This is a strange kind of personage whom we see.

2. A character of the party inquired about. It is a woman, one of the weak sex, as the church of believers is represented in scripture. She is not one of the dwellers in the wilderness. She appears not to have built her house there. She is but a traveller through it, and her head is awayward from it; and she is set for another country. That is she whom we mean, who is coming up from the wilderness. I make no question but by the wilderness here is meant

---

* The substance of several sermons preached at Ettrick, June 18, 1721, and subsequent Sabbaths.

the world, as Cant. iii. 6; and iv. 8; with a plain eye to the Israelites coming through the wilderness to Canaan; the last of which, as it was typical of heaven, so the former is of the world.

But for the further understanding of these words, it is necessary to take notice of a custom among the Jews at their marriages, to which there is here a manifest allusion, viz., The bridegroom used to take his bride, and carry her out of the city into the fields, and there they had their nuptial-songs; and afterward he brought her back again, leaning on him, into the city, to his father's house, and there the marriage was solemnized. Now we may be sure, however, that these fields were not a wilderness or moorlands, no fit place for a bridegroom and bride's walk together. This, then, increases the wonder, What a bride is this that is coming up out of the wilderness with her Bridegroom, leaning on him? Others use to be entertained more softly and delicately; what a bride and Bridegroom are these! However, here is represented the Christian life, the life of the church of believers espoused to Christ. In which observe two things.

1*st*, Her exercise; she is travelling upon her road away with her espoused husband, namely, Christ. The place she is going from is the wilderness-world; the place she is going to appears, from what is said, to be her Bridegroom's Father's house. Her way is upward, her motion an ascending, as the word imports; and here should rather be read "going up," than "coming up," as Judg. xx. 21, since the decency of the parable requires it, she being rather going from the place where the daughters of Jerusalem were, than to the place where they were.

2*dly*, Her posture, her travelling posture; "leaning on her Beloved." This is what in New Testament language is called the life of faith; for that is the spiritual leaning of the soul, and imports a fiducial persuasion. It bears, (1.) Her having her Bridegroom's company through the wilderness. He leaves her not there alone; he bids her go nowhere but where he himself will go with her. (2.) Her having his help through the wilderness. She leans on him, as a weak woman on a journey leans upon her husband.

Three doctrines offer themselves from the words.

DOCT. I. True believers, espoused to Christ, turning their back on the world, and walking heavenward with him, are a mystery, a strange sight in the world. Who is this!

DOCT. II. The life of believers, as espoused to Christ, is a going up from the wilderness of this world, with him, to his Father's house in the heavenly Canaan.

Doct. III. The way to get up from the wilderness-world to the heavenly Canaan, is to go all along leaning on Jesus Christ by faith.

I shall illustrate and apply the first two of these doctrines distinctly, and consider the third in a word of direction in the application of the second.

Doct. I. True believers, espoused to Christ, turning their back on the world, and walking heavenward with him, are a mystery, a strange sight in the world. Who is this!

In discoursing this subject I shall,

I. Premise some things for right understanding the doctrine.

II. Shew in what respects believers are a mystery, a strange sight in the world.

III. Give the reasons of the point.

IV. Apply.

I. I shall premise some things for right understanding the doctrine.

1. Sin turned this world into an enemy's country in respect of heaven, and so into a wilderness. It was originally the seat of the friend of God, the confederate of heaven, innocent Adam; and then it was a pleasant land. But sin entering, it changed masters, so that the devil is become the god of this world, 2 Cor. iv. 4, and it a wilderness because the primitive communication betwixt heaven and it is stopped, and a new one settled betwixt hell and this world.

2. All men by their first birth are natives of this world; their father's house is in it, the people of it are the people that are theirs, Psalm xlv. 10. And home is home, be it never so homely; they love the wilderness, they desire not to change, they know no better country, and they seek none better. They are pleased with the place, the company, and the manner of living; for they are all natural to them.

3. The Lord from eternity having set his love upon some of the natives, in due time comes in the gospel into the wilderness-world, and making love to them, gains their consent, and is espoused to them in the everlasting marriage-covenant, according to Hos. ii. 19, "I will betroth thee unto me for ever, yea, I will betroth thee unto me in righteousness, and in judgment, and in loving-kindness, and in mercies." Isa. xliv. 5, "One shall say, I am the Lord's." Thus he becomes theirs, and they his, and they are engaged to follow him whithersoever he goes. Not only are they obliged by their contract of espousals to go with him, but their hearts are so set upon him, that they cannot think of parting with him again, or staying behind him.

4. Though the espousals and the feasts of espousals are held in the wilderness, yet the place set for the consummating of the marriage is Christ's Father's house in Cannan above, to which he begins immediately to carry his bride. She must no longer be a residenter in the world, a dweller in the wilderness, but must lift her heart and affections off her own people, and her father's house, and be going away homeward to Christ's Father's house, that the marriage may be consummated.

5. This her going away up from the wilderness with her espoused Husband, is a going away in heart and affections; it is the soul's motion heavenwards in this life, the last step of which is made at death. It is a gracious frame of heart shining forth in a holy, tender, and heavenly walk. Every step in the way of holiness, in mortification, vivification, and contempt of the world, is a step homeward to Christ's Father's house.

6. *Lastly.* Christ's bride at her waygoing, and ongoing with him thus, is a mystery, a strange sight in the world. Her own country-people gaze at her, to see her undertaking such a strange journey, turning her back on the beloved world, and setting out for a strange country. Sometimes believers fall out of the exercise of grace, become untender in their walk, and grow so like the world, that they do not appear to be going up out of the wilderness, but rather pitching their tents there. But when they are in the exercise of grace, holy and heavenly in their walk, then do the spectators make the question, " Who is this ?" Like the Jewish rulers, who " seeing the boldness of Peter and John, and perceiving that they were ignorant and unlearned men, marvelled, and took knowledge of them, that they had been with Jesus ;" Acts iv. 13.

II. I shall show in what respects believers are a mystery, a strange sight in the world; the power of godliness appearing in their walk at this rate, so that it is said of them, " Who is this ?"

1. There is something very amiable about them, as we are told of the primitive Christians; Acts ii. 46, 47, that " they continuing daily with one accord in the temple, and breaking bread from house to house, did eat their meat with gladness and singleness of heart, praising God, and having favour with all the people." There is a conscience within worldly men, as well as corruption; and what their corruptions will condemn, their conscience will approve as lovely; 2 Cor. iv. 2. Men's corruptions may get the management of their tongue, hands, and their whole external behaviour, and may set the man to run down piety, and the party in whom it appears; yet in the meantime conscience within their breasts will be applauding and admiring the godly man, as one who has something very lovely

about him, as Balaam did in the case of the Israelites; Numb. xxiii. 9, 10.

2. There is something very awful about them to beholders. Paul stands at the bar and reasons, and Felix sitting on the bench trembles; Acts xxiv. 25. John Baptist lies in his grave beheaded at Herod's command, and yet there he is a terror to Herod; Matth. xiv. 1, 2. The remains of God's image on man in point of dominion, has an awe and majesty with it, that affects the brutes; Gen. ix. 2. How much more has the restored image of God in righteousness and holiness shining forth in a Christian's life, a majesty with it, procuring an internal reverence to them from beholders! They are to them like men of another world, and every view they take of such writes death to them; Heb. xi. 7.

3. There is something very mysterious about them; Zech. iii. 8. They are like foreigners in a country, apt to become a gazing-stock, a wonder, about which the natives cannot satisfy themselves. A believer marching heavenward, away from this wilderness-world, is,

(1.) A mystery to the men of the world, whether professors or profane. They cannot comprehend them, for they are God's "hidden ones;" Psalm lxxxiii. 3, not hid from their bodily eyes; ver. 4, but from the eyes of their minds. What a mystery is that man to them, who sets his feet and treads on that, which they set their hearts on and adore? who values, pursues eagerly, and by no means can be brought to part with, that which they can see no beauty in? whose principles, aims, and actions are diametrically opposite to those of theirs? They are to them like men of another mould and make, which they cannot understand. Nay, they are,

(2.) A mystery to themselves, ay, so great many times, that they know not what to make of themselves, what class to rank themselves in, whether of saints or sinners; Psalm cxxxix. 23, 24. A true Christian is indeed a bundle of mysteries; he on earth, and his head in heaven, yet really and truly united! John xv. 5; crucified with Christ, yet living; living, yet not he, but Christ living in him, Gal. ii. 20; not loitering, but labouring, yet not he, but "the grace of God with him;" 1 Cor. xv. 10. He is a man of two leading contrary principles, having a will and not a will to one and the same thing; he sins, and yet it is not he; Rom. vii. 17. He has many spots and stains on him, yet is all fair; Cant. iv. 7; "black, yet comely, as the tents of Kedar, as the curtains of Solomon;" chap. i. 5; wanting many things, yet complete; Col. ii. 10. What wonder that such a one should be in way of admiration inquired about, "Who is this?"

III. I shall give the reasons of the point, That true believers are a mystery, a strange sight in the world.

1. Because they are so unlike the world, they are like speckled birds among the rest, 1 Pet. iv. 4. They are cast into the new mould of regeneration, and are come forth nonconformists to the world, Rom. xii. 2. They have got another spirit, than the spirit which all their people and their father's house are acted by, which casts their whole conversation into quite another shape than theirs, Num. xiv. 24. So the unlikeness betwixt them makes them a strange sight.

2. Because they are so unlike themselves in former times. Saul among the prophets was a strange sight, 1 Sam. x. 11. But the grace of God makes a more wonderful change in a man from what he was before, as appears in Saul among the apostles, 1 Tim. i. 12, 13. What an observable change was there, that he which persecuted the saints in times past, now preacheth the faith which once he destroyed! Gal. i. 23. Grace makes lambs of lions, casts out the dumb devil, that they who cared not for praying, preaching, &c. but all these things were a burden to them, they cannot for the world live without them. It makes a new heart, a new life, a new man, all things new, 2 Cor. v. 17.

3. Because they are very rare in the world; they are but here and there one for a marvel, Jer. iii. 14. The multitude in the world prefer the wilderness to Zion, and sit still in their native land, and will not go away with Christ. They have the gospel-call, they are courted to match with Christ; but they think gospel-invitations but idle tales, and they have beloveds of their own in the wilderness, which they will not part with for him. Some say with the mouth they will take him, and subscribe with the hand at solemn ordinances; but it is not a match, for their hearts were never truly for it; so they sit still too, and go not up with him out of the wilderness, but their carcases fall there. So that they who are going up out of the wilderness, being so rare, are a strange sight.

Use I. of information. It informs us, that,

1. Serious souls need not think it strange, if they become a wonder to many, Psalm lxxi. 7. They are not meet to go up with Christ from the wilderness, that are not content to become a world's wonder for him. They must be fools for Christ that will be wise; Mark viii. ult., " Whosoever shall be ashamed of me, and of my words, in this adulterous and sinful generation, of him also shall the Son of man be ashamed, when he cometh in the glory of his Father, with the holy angels." Worldly men wonder at seriousness now, what makes the saints so nice in points of truth and holiness; but that wonder will not last long, the world will soon see they had good reason for it all.

2. The world is no idle spectator of those who have given themselves to Christ, and profess to follow him. They take notice of them, and have their questions about them. Communicants, take heed to yourselves; many eyes are on you, as to your after-walk; God's eye is on you; the world's eyes will be upon you, they will take notice whether ye turn your back on the world, the ways and manners of it, or even sit still with themselves as before.

3. Those who shall still walk after the course of the world, continue sons of earth, not making away heavenward in the tenor of their life and conversation, are not espoused to Christ; though they have given him the hand, they have not given him the heart. The sincerity of your covenanting with God is now to be proved by your after-walk. If God be your Father, be setting homeward to his house. If Christ be your espoused husband, make away with him through the wilderness, and stay not behind. The friendship of the world is enmity with God.

4. *Lastly.* This world must be little worth, wherein, among such multitudes, there are so few such travellers, that they are a strange sight. There are many sad sights to be seen in the world, even after communions, but few of this sort of persons turning their backs on the world, and resolutely walking heavenwards. Take heed, Christians and communicants, that one of these three questions be not put concerning you, instead of this in the text. (1.) Who is this standing still in the wilderness? like the door on the hinges, oft moving, but never going forward, as proud, passionate, carnal, and sensual, as before? Isa. v. 6. (2.) Who is this going back from the wilderness to Egypt, to the flesh-pots there? back again to their profane and licentious courses? better ye had never known the way of righteousness. (3.) Who is this sticking in some mire, fallen into some pit in the wilderness; some gross and scandalous abomination? Many such trophy gets Satan set up.

Use II. Of exhortation. O Christians, communicants, walk so as the world may bear witness, that ye are going up out of the wilderness, leaning on your beloved; that your faces and hearts are heavenward; that ye have set off from them, and are no more theirs.

This would be much to the honour of Christ and religion, Acts iv. 13. It would be a great kindness to the world lying in wickedness, as an apt mean to bring others away with you, Zech. viii. *ult.* It would be the safety and comfort of your own souls, Cant. viii. 4.

Ye will walk so, if ye be habitually heavenly in the frame of your heart, like Enoch walking with God. Also, if in your conversation ye manifest a contempt of the world: *Germana illa bestia non curat aurum,* was Luther's character from his enemies. Likewise, if ye be just in your dealings in the world to a niceness, counting it always safer to lose a pound, than unjustly gain a small penny. And further, if ye be clothed with humility and with humanity, meek, ruling your own spirit, doing good to all, even to those that wrong you; and are patient under trouble, and living by faith.

DOCT. II. The life of believers as espoused to Christ, is a going up from the wilderness of this world, with him, to his Father's house in the heavenly Canaan.

In discoursing from this doctrine, I shall,

I. Take notice of some things supposed in it.

II. Unfold the believer's life, as a going up from the wilderness of this world, typified by the Israelites going up from the wilderness to Canaan.

III. Make application.

I. I shall take notice of some things supposed in this doctrine. It supposes, that,

1. As soon as a soul is espoused to Christ, it is loosed from the world. Its taking of him is a letting this world go, Matth. xiii. 44. The unbeliever hugs and embraces this world as his portion, and pursues it as the main thing; but when he closeth with Christ he saith, "Thou art my portion," and the esteem of the world sinks, Phil. iii. 8. Those that are espoused to Christ, are,

(1.) A loosed people. The bands with which the world held them are loosed; they gripe not it, nor it them, at the rate they formerly grasped one the other, Gal. vi. 14. While the sinner was without Christ, the profits and pleasures of the world were strong bands, which they could not get shaken off; but in the day of the power of converting grace, these give way, as tow does when touched with the fire. Then Christ says, "Loose him and let him go;" all is nothing in comparison of Christ.

(2.) A separated people. Though before they made one body with the world lying in wickedness, and were possessed with the same spirit of the world; yet in the day of their espousals to Christ, they are fairly separated from them, 2 Cor. vi. 17, even as a married woman ceases to be any more a member of her father's family, but becomes a member of her husband's, Psalm xlv. 10.

(3.) A new people. They are no more men of the world, though in it, Psalm xvii. 14, but heavenly men, 1 Cor. xv. 48. They have another spirit, Numb. xiv. 24, a new principle, ends, motives, and manner of life.

2. The soul espoused to Christ, being loosed from the world, is set in motion heavenwards, away from the world, Psalm lxxxiv. 5—7. That soul has begun a new journey, is set off in the Christian race,

that it may obtain the crown. Those that are in heaven have come to a fixed point of happiness; those in hell have come to a fixed point in misery; as to those that are in the wilderness of this world some of them are sitting still as in Sodom, till the fire of God fall on them and consume them; others, even true believers, are making away, as Lot out of Sodom, and as the Israelites out of the wilderness into Canaan.

3. The believer's journeying heavenwards is attended with many difficulties. It is an up-going, and that through a wilderness. They that mind for heaven must forego their own ease, and lay their account with troubles and trials of many sorts. The way to destruction is broad and easy; if men will but sit still, they will be carried quickly down the stream into the ocean of an eternity of wo. But if one minds for heaven, he must force his way, through many difficulties, Matth. vii. 13, 14, and xi. 12.

4. The believer's passage to heaven is also a work of time. It is not a leaping out of the wilderness into Canaan, but a going up out of it by degrees. It cost Israel long forty years in the wilderness. And the believer is longer or shorter kept in the wilderness, as seems meet to his God. Some are not long set upon the way, when they are at their journey's end; others it costs many a weary look to be at home.

5. Christ is with the believer in the journey. It is a weary land they have to go through, but they are not alone in it, Cant. iv. 8. In the day the soul is espoused to Christ, he is united to him spiritually, and that union once made is never broken again. So that wherever it is the believer's lot to go, Christ is with him, if it were through fire and water, Isa. xliii. 2. He is never so far from him, but that his faith may get hold of him, and he may lean on him.

6. *Lastly*. The end of this journey is a most comfortable one. Though the travelling be uneasy, the designed place of rest *is most* desirable, being Christ's Father's house, where the marriage is to be solemnized for ever, John xiv. 2. This is sufficient to bear up the heart of Christ's spouse through all the difficulties of the road, Heb. xi. 26, especially considering that Christ himself goes all along with her, Heb. xiii. 5.

II. I shall unfold the believer's life, as a going up from the wilderness of this world, typified by the Israelites going up from the wilderness to Canaan. And here I shall shew,

1. How they are brought unto the wilderness.
2. How the believer is set into it.
3. How he is going up from it.
4. The hardships and inconveniencies of the road.
5. The advantages and conveniencies of it.

First, I shall shew you how believers are brought unto the wilderness. The world is not a wilderness to them and in their esteem, till they be brought out of the Egyptian bondage of their natural state. Then, and not till then, they enter into their wilderness-state, And here one may remark these six things.

1. As the Israelites who came out of Egypt, went down into it in the loins of their fathers; so the elect of God were brought into their sinful and miserable state in the loins of our first father Adam, Rom. v. 12. And we are all born in that condition, and draw our first breath in that unhappy region.

2. The natural state of the elect is a state of bondage and slavery. Satan, as Pharaoh, is their prince there, and holds them fast at their drudgery, Eph. ii. 2, 3. They have many taskmasters there; as many reigning lusts as there are in their hearts, so many taskmasters are there holding them to their work.

3. As God, by the hand of Moses the lawgiver, and Aaron the high-priest, wrought the deliverance of the Israelites; so, by the law and the gospel, he carries on the deliverance of the elect out of their state of bondage. The law serves to awaken the sinner, and shew him his danger; the gospel discovers the remedy; and the Spirit of God makes both effectual.

4. There is no less opposition made by Satan to the sinner's deliverance from his spiritual bondage, than was by Pharaoh to the deliverance of the Israelites. He is loath to lose his subjects, loath to let his prisoners go. How often does the field seem to be won, and a fair appearance that the poor sinners shall be let go? and yet there are new attacks to be made before he will surrender.

5. Ordinarily, whenever the deliverance is set a-foot, the bondage becomes harder than ever before, Rom. vii. 9. Satan then musters up all his forces, and rages more than ever, that he may make the soul despair of a delivery. Now is the soul hard bestead, duties are bound on by the law laid to the conscience, under the pain of the curse, but no strength afforded; so the soul sees it must make brick while no straw is given. And by this means their corruptions are irritated, that they appear more vigorously than ever before, Rom. vii. 5.

6. *Lastly*. But at the set time, over the belly of all opposition, God brings his elect out of their spiritual bondage into the wilderness. There is a set time in the purpose of God for the delivery of every elect soul; and as at the appointed time precisely Israel was delivered, Exod. xii. 41, so are they, Jer. ii. 24. And no sooner do they comply with the gospel-call, and leave the spiritual Egypt, but as soon this world turns a wilderness unto them. And young con-

verts may lay their account with a hot pursuit from Satan to bring them back again, even as sure as the Israelites met with it from Pharaoh. But they may be assured that they shall get such a deliverance as the Israelites at the Red Sea, which shall make them sing.

Secondly, I shall shew how the believer is set into the wilderness. When once converting grace has made a fair separation betwixt the sinner and the world, presently he enters into a wilderness-state.

1. He cares not for the world as he was wont, Gal. vi. 14. Grace opening the eyes the world appears in its own colours, no more a fruitful field but a barren wilderness. The most pleasant spots in it appear lions' dens and mountains of leopards. Its best fruits appear as the apples of Sodom, fair to look at, but being handled fall to ashes, Psalm iv. 6, 7. He sees there is no rest for his heart in it, and therefore must look above and beyond it. The men of the world are no more his choice; their way and manner of life he can no more away with.

2. The world cares not for him as before, Gal. vi. 14. No sooner does a soul begin to look heavenward, but presently the world turns a strange world to him, John xv. 19. He must be content to dwell alone, and not to be reckoned among the nations. He bears the image which they hate, he is entered on a course opposite to theirs; and so the friendship breaks up. And he may lay his account with all the opposition they can make him with tongue and hand.

3. Then it becomes, by God's appointment, the place of trial for him, as the wilderness was to the Israelites, Deut. viii. 2. God could have taken his people a nearer way to Canaan than the way he led them; but for their trial he led them so long in the wilderness. So he could carry each believer straightway to heaven after their conversion; but he will have them pass their trials before they come there; so they must be content to take up their cross and follow him, and so long stand candidates for glory, while one trial is put to them after another; trials that will prove the reality and strength of their graces, the multiplicity of their corruptions and remaining vigour of them.

4. *Lastly*. It is no more his home or his rest; but the place of his pilgrimage, of his sojourning, the place he must travel through in his way home to his eternal rest, Heb. xi. 13. He must look on himself as upon a journey, one that is not to stay here, but must be going forward to the heavenly country.

Thirdly, I shall shew how the believer is going up from the wilderness; he is going up from it,

1. By the course of nature, which is swift as a post, a ship, and as an eagle's flight. It is but a little time, and believers will be at

their journey's end. Every day sets them a good way nearer their eternal rest, Rom. xiii. 11. If the days be evil, they are but few, and will soon be over. It is true that by this way the wicked are going out from the world too, but they are not going up, but down into destruction.

2. In the habitual bent of his heart and affections. Believers' hearts are turned off the world, and set on things above. Their face is homeward, their heart is there before them; for Christ is there, their treasure is there. Hence they are said to be those who love Christ's appearing, 2 Tim. iv. 8; and look for him, Heb. ix. 28. So when the carnal man is glued to this world, and desires no better heaven than what is here, they are going away from it in affection and desire.

But it may be the case of some gracious souls, that they cannot say they are thus going up from the world, nay, it is a terror to them to think of going out of it. I answer, there is a twofold desire to be away from the world, and to be with Christ. (1.) There is an explicit desire, like a rose full spread. Such was that of Paul; Phil. i. 23, "I desire to depart, and to be with Christ." This is found in believers, when they are not only in the exercise of grace, but have a full assurance of their eternal salvation. This makes the soul go up with full sail out of the world. (2.) An implicit desire which is like a rose-bud, where the leaves are to be found, if it be opened, though in the meantime they are covered, not being yet so ripe as to spread. This is found in believers, if they be at all in the exercise of grace, although they be in the dark as to their state. It is found in the groaning believer, who is groaning under the remains of sin, and would fain be free from them, groaning under want of communion with God, and would fain have it, and that so as not to be interrupted any more, Rom. vii. 24. The Lord reads the language of these groans so, and there wants only a full assurance of eternal happiness to make it plain language to the soul itself. See 2 Cor. v. 4. And thus the believer is going up from the wilderness, though with the wind in his face.

3. In progressive sanctification; Prov. iv. 18. By faith the soul is set on the way to Immanuel's land; it knits him to Christ the personal way, it sets him to holiness of heart and life, the real way, or the walking in the way; Col. ii. 6. And the believer goes on while he goes forward in holiness, especially when he is growing, adding a cubit to his spiritual stature; 2 Pet. iii. *ult.* This going up appears,

(1.) In mortification, when the believer is dying to sin, getting his former lusts weakened; Rom. viii. 13. Mortification is the daily task of a believer; the weeds of corruption in the heart are never so plucked up, but they will be ready to sprout again. These Canaanites are left in the land, that the believer may never be idle, but watch their motions and bear them down.

(2.) In vivification, in living to righteousness, when the soul holds forward in the way of duty over the belly of all opposition, especially in a holy and heavenly frame, going on in them with vigour, whether it be doing-work or suffering-work; Cant. iii. 6. The soul married to Christ is to be for him, according to the law of marriage, Hos. iii. 3. As we live by him, so we must live to him. This was Paul's practice; Phil. i. 21, "To me to live is Christ." More particularly,

4. In obtaining victory over the world; 1 John v. 4. The world is an enemy to all that are set to go up from it. And many times it prevails to retard their course; they are in it travelling in a stony, yea and thorny way, where there are many things to take hold of them, and hold them still; so that they are in hazard of being entangled in the wilderness.

In this respect a believer goes up from the wilderness. And O but the picture of a believer thus going up from the wilderness is a beautiful one; Cant. iii. 6, "Who is this that cometh out of the wilderness like pillars of smoke, perfumed with myrrh and frankincense, with all powders of the merchant?" I shall essay to draw it in a few particulars. A believer espoused to Christ, and thus going up from the wilderness-world, is,

1. One who is keeping off from mixing with the men of the world, the natives of the weary land. Converting grace plucks them out from among them, and sets them over to Christ's side; and establishing grace keeps them from mixing again; Psalm xii. 7. There is a generation of God's wrath in the world, and they are labouring to save themselves from them; Acts ii. 40. They are deserters of their company, shunning unnecessary fellowship with them; for they know, that "a companion of fools shall be destroyed;" Prov. xiii. 20. And they consort with those who are followers of the Lamb, companions of those that fear God.

2. He is holding off from the ways of the world; Psalm xvii. 4. In the wilderness-world there are many ways, all of them leading to and terminating in some part of the wilderness; some to the world's wealth, honours, peace, &c. But there is one way that leads out of it, terminates in the heavenly Canaan. The throng of the world goes in these many ways; but the believers, and they only, take the pilgrim's way, which does but lie through it, neither beginning nor ending in the country; and the grass may grow on it

for the natives, and they never set a foot on it; Isa. xxxv. 8. The men of the world ply them to turn them aside, and take their way; and if they catch them napping, they readily get them off; but the traveller towards Zion says as Israel to the king of Edom, "We will go by the king's highway, we will not turn to the right hand nor to the left;" Numb. xx. 17.

3. He has a low estimate of the world's wisdom, and holds off from it as from a false light that would lead the traveller into a quagmire; 1 Cor. iii. 18, 19. Carnal wisdom has often been the ruin of Christ's interests in the church, and in the private case of Christians; leading into a betraying of truth and purity; procuring outward peace, but wounding one's conscience, and dishonouring God. But they that are going up from the wilderness, will be no admirers of the world's judgment in the matter of truth and error, sin and duty; for the generality of men have ever been, and will be, in that case, blind men judging of colours. And it is a dangerous thing to be carried away with the stream; Eph. ii. 2. A man that has no heart to keep off a way, because it is a way that is in vogue in the world, and will always row with the stream, is not going up from the wilderness. The fear of the world's putting the fool's cap on one's head, makes many a carcase fall in the wilderness.

4. He is keeping up a holy contempt of the world's good things; Heb. xi. 24, 25. Its profits and pleasures are sinking in their value with him; he "counts them but loss and dung, that he may win Christ;" Phil. iii. 8. To a gracious soul going up from the wilderness, the best things the world can afford, are so lightly esteemed, that he will not think them worth pains to go off the King's highway for them; Numb. xx. 17, "We will not pass through the fields, or through the vineyards, neither will we drink of the water of the wells;" while others allured with these baits, fall into one mire after another, and quit the travelling company, as Demas did Paul.

5. He is resolute to make his way through the world's ill things, to follow the way of God through good and bad report, Rev. xiv. 4. He is neither to be bribed nor boasted by the world out of the way of his duty; Cant. viii. 7, "Many waters cannot quench love, neither can the floods drown it; if a man would give all the substance of his house for love, it would utterly be contemned." His feet are shod with the preparation of the gospel of peace, and blow what weather it will, he must hold on till he be at his journey's end.

6. *Lastly*. His eyes are upon the other world; they are fixed on the prize, and running that they may obtain it, Heb. xi. 26. Their conversation is in heaven; they are habitually minding heavenly

things; their affections are set not on things on the earth, but on the things that are above. But I proceed to consider,

Fourthly, The hardships and inconveniencies of the wilderness-road, which the believer must lay his account with, while he goes up from the wilderness.

1. It is a weary land which the traveller has to go through, while he is going up from the wilderness, Isa. xxxii. 2. David calls the whole of it, the house of his pilgrimage. However lightly the natives, the men of the earth, may live in it, there is never one born from above that is travelling through it, but it is a weary land to them. It was a weary time the Israelites had of it in the wilderness; their patience soon began to wear out. And there is never a child of God, but sometime or other he has his fill of it, and being wearied, longs to be at home. The Son of God himself, we find, wearied here, John iv. 6.

2. It is a road that lies through a waste, affording no provision, Deut. xxxii. 10. When sin entered into the world, a withering curse followed on the back of sin, and turned the pleasant land into a waste, barren place. There was a blessing in everything in it before, but now everything is embittered in it. There is enough to raise the appetite of lusts, there are husks enough for them to feed on; but there is nothing in it to fill the soul, that is the produce of the country; and therefore the natives, though they are always feeding, they are never full. The Israelites would have starved in the wilderness, if they had not been furnished from another quarter; for there was neither meat nor drink there for them.

3. It is an howling wilderness which they have to go through, Deut. xxxii. 10, because of the wild beasts that haunt there, Cant. iv. 8, devils, and wicked men influenced by the devil. Sometimes the traveller must hear them roaring, Psalm lxxiv. 4, threatening to devour and swallow them up, and to make the name of Israel no more to be remembered, as the Egyptian wild beast did, Exod. xv. 9, "I will pursue, I will overtake, I will divide the spoil: my lust shall be satisfied upon them, I will draw my sword, my hand shall destroy them." Sometimes he is entertained with their yellings, Jer. ii. 15. Their blasphemies, reproaches against God and his cause, their contradicting of the truths of religion, what are they but yellings of the wilderness, as ungrateful to holy ears as the yellings of beasts in the night? Sometimes he must find them tearing him, his name, reputation, substance, yea and his flesh sometimes, Psalm xxxv. 15, 16.

4. They must lay their account with scorching heats in it. Such was the wilderness to Israel, for which a cloud covered them by day. While they are upon the road through the wilderness, they are liable

to fiery heats of desertion from heaven; to fiery heats of temptation from hell, Eph. vi. 16, fiery trials of persecution from men, 1 Pet. iv. 12, and fiery heats of contention and division, the fire coming from the altar, Rev. viii. 5. All which make travelling Zionward to be very hard; and the more hard, the greater these heats are; which puts the spouse of Christ to that prayer, Cant. i. 7, "Tell me, O thou whom my soul loveth, where thou feedest, where thou makest thy flock to rest at noon."

5. It is a sickly place through which their way lieth. Many a groan was in the wilderness while Israel was in it; sometimes there were fiery serpents biting them, and sometimes a plague consuming them, so as many carcases fell in the wilderness. No less sickly a place is this world to the spiritual travellers. It is a heavy disease that is on them there, even a whole body of death, Rom. vii. 24. It affects and indisposes the whole man. They are liable to frequent relapses; and O the malignant influence it has on their journey, unfitting them for it, and at best causing them to go up but very slowly!

6. It is a difficult way through the wilderness. The road the travellers must go will try their patience, their strength, &c. They that must needs have an easy way through the wilderness, must take the way that leads down to the pit, not the way that leads up to Immanuel's land.

(1.) It is all upward, which scares most men at it, Psalm xxiv. 3, "Who shall ascend into the hill of the Lord? The way to heaven is up the hill, the way to hell down the hill.

(2.) It is a narrow way, Matth. vii. 14. Multitudes walk in the broad way, and there they get room enough, life-room, heart-room, conscience-room. But the King's highway has no such room in it, which obliges the travellers to take good heed to their feet, Eph. v. 15. And considering how rash we are naturally, how weak-headed, false-hearted, how narrow the road is, how loose the ground about it is, it is no great wonder that many of the travellers catch such falls, as make them go halting to the grave, Psalm li. 8.

(3.) It is a hard and rugged way; and therefore they must have leg-hardness, as soldiers had to preserve their feet from stones and roughness in the way of their march; Eph. vi. 15. There are many difficulties to go through, which will need resolution and undaunted courage.

(4.) It is a way wherein many snares are laid for them. In every lot in the world, and in the most innocent things, there are snares wherewith we may be caught. And sometimes men are busy making snares for us in the way wherein we walk.

7. It is a very solitary road, there is not much company to be got in it; Matth. vii. 14. Israel travelled alone through the wilderness, save that a mixed multitude joined with them, that they were much the worse of, and whose carcases fell in the wilderness. See how Micaiah complains for want of company on the road, "Wo is me? for I am as when they have gathered the summer fruits, as the grape-gleanings of the vintage; there is no cluster to eat; my soul desired the first ripe-fruit;" Micah vii. 1. In Elijah's days there were so very few upon the road, that he thought he had been alone upon it; he had so little help of the seven thousand, that he knew not of them; Rom. xi. 3, 4. At this rate the spiritual traveller has few.

(1.) To take a lift of his burden; Gal. vi. 2. Alas! we are in a strange world, where there are many to lay a load above the burden, but few to take a lift of it.

(2.) To consult with when he comes to a difficult step. There are many such steps that Christians will meet with in their way to Zion, especially when a mist rises in the wilderness. And it is no small mercy to have honest and tender men to advise with, and to have their sympathy and prayers. But of all these there is great scarcity in the wilderness.

8. *Lastly,* It is a road, wherein they must meet with armed enemies come forth to attack them, and ruin them. Pharaoh and his army pursued the Israelites in the wilderness; Exod. xiv. 3. Amalek fought them, chap. xvii. 8, both types of the devil and his agents. The Christian life is a fighting life; 2 Tim. iv. 7. All is not done when they are converted, they must fight their way through the wilderness to Canaan, and so fight as to overcome; Rev. iii. 21. The concluding of their peace with God in Christ, is proclaiming of war against the devil, the world, and the flesh; so they must put on their armour, if they would make their way through the wilderness.

Fifthly, I now come to show the advantages and conveniencies of the wilderness-road. The people of God, while in the wilderness-world, have as much allowed them from heaven as may balance the hardships of the wilderness.

1. The pillar of cloud to go before them in the wilderness; of which we have an account; Exod. xiii. 20, 21, 22, "And they took their journey from Succoth, and encamped in Etham, in the edge of the wilderness. And the Lord went before them by day in a pillar of a cloud, to lead them the way: and by night in a pillar of fire, to give them light; to go by day and night. He took not away the pillar of the cloud by day nor the pillar of fire by night, from before the people." It was a type of Christ. He leaves them not alone in

the wilderness-world. Our Lord Christ is upon the head of the travelling company, Cant. iv. 8; and will be so till he have them all home. And this is sufficient to compensate the solitariness of the way.

The pillar seems to have been a fiery cloud, Exod. xiv. 20; the cloud representing Christ's human nature, the fire his divine nature; and to have been but one pillar; Numb. ix. 15, 16; Christ one person in two distinct natures. A God vailed with flesh, is the believer's company in the wilderness at all times; and even the man Christ travelled the wilderness-road himself too.

It had a dark side to their enemies, but a light side to the Israelites, Exod xiv. 20. Believers see a glory in Christ which the blind world sees nothing of, and therefore will not go up with him from the wilderness. The carnal world wonders at the believer's way-going from the wilderness; alas! they see not what he sees, the light side of the cloud goes before.

Now the cloudy pillar had a fourfold use to the Israelites in the wilderness, in a spiritual sense made good by Christ to his people in the wilderness-world.

(1.) They had the signal for marching or halting from it, Numb. ix. 17, &c. Their motions were directed by its motions. Thus the travellers from the wilderness-world are directed by Jesus Christ their Lord and Head, on whom the trust of bringing them safe to glory is devolved; Isa. lv. 4, "Behold, I have given him for —a leader and commander to the people." They must not stir till he give them the sign, though all the world, friends or foes, should cry, March; if they presume to do it, the cloud of glory will stay behind them, and they will find themselves entangled in the wilderness. They must not sit still when he gives them the sign to march, though all the world, friends or enemies, should cry, Halt; if they do, they will find the glory of the Lord will leave them, and their rest be blasted. Here lies their safety in the wilderness, in observing the word from heaven.

(2.) It led them in the way, Exod. xiii. 21. They would soon have missed their way in the pathless wilderness. So our Lord Christ leads his people in their way through the wilderness-world, Isa. lv. 4. In the wilderness there are many by-ways, many to lead the travellers off the way, besides a wandering disposition in their own nature. They will never get through safe, who take the guiding of themselves; but they who keep their eye on the cloud of glory before them, shall get through the most difficult steps of the wilderness-road, Prov. iii. 5, 6.

He leads his people through the wilderness, (1.) By his word, which they must take good heed to, as that which determines the way, Isa. xxx. 21. By his word he chalks out the path through the wilderness, and whatever agrees not therewith is but a by-way, it is not the King's highway, Isa. viii. 20, "To the law and to the testimony; if they speak not according to this word, it is because there is no light in them." (2.) By his example, which is the marks of his own feet upon the way, 1 Pet. ii. 21. These we should narrowly observe, that we may follow them; hence says our Lord himself; Matth. xi. 29, "Learn of me, for I am meek and lowly in heart." We are apt to follow example; whose example should be so dear to us as his, who is our Father, Master, Husband? &c. That we might know how to walk through the wilderness, God himself came down from heaven, and in our nature walked through it. (3.) By his providence, which, duly compared with the word, contributes much to clear the way; Psalm xxxii. 8, "I will instruct thee and teach thee in the way which thou shalt go; I will guide thee with mine eye." Ye are to be then careful observers of providences, which are really waymarks in the wilderness, Psalm cvii. *ult.* (4.) By his Spirit, which renders all the rest effectual; John xvi. 13, "When he the Spirit of truth is come, he will guide you into all truth." He illuminates and causes to shine, the word, Christ's example, and providences. He illuminates the traveller too, as well as the way; disposes, moves, and efficaciously leads the traveller on his way.

(3.) It was a shelter to them from the heat of the sun by day; Psalm cv. 39. And so Christ shelters his people from the scorching heats in the wilderness; Isa. xxii. 2, and iv. 6. Let the heat of desertion, temptation, contention with men, and persecution, be never so great; Christ looked to by faith will be a sufficient sconce; Cant. i. 7. Many a time the gourds of created comforts are withered when the sun is hottest in the wilderness. Sons of men are found vanity and a lie. But Christ's shadow is ever broad and refreshing; Cant ii. 3, and the traveller can never come amiss to it.

(4.) It was a light to them by night, Exod. xiii. 21. There is many a dark night in the wilderness; and it is sometimes the lot of the people of God to travel in the night, as well as it was that of Israel, Numb. ix. 21. But Christ is a light to them in the darkest hour of the night; hence David could say, Psalm xxiii. 4, "Yea, though I walk through the valley of the shadow of death, I will fear no evil: for thou art with me, thy rod and thy staff they comfort me." Sometimes the sun shines fair, and then there is no debate about the way: at other times a mist and darkness sits down in the wilderness, and then many are put to a stand; then is a time of wandering, stumbling, falling over this and the other precipice in the wilderness.

Many are lying fallen, and others come up and fall over them; and all because of the darkness. What way can one get through in such a time? Why, let them keep their eye on Christ the pillar of fire, and they shall have light in the midst of darkness, Job xxix. 3.

2. They have provision allowed them from heaven in the waste wilderness. And that must balance the scarcity and want there. The King's country affords them provision for their journey. Israel in the wilderness were provided both with meat and drink; and so are they that are going up from the wilderness of this world. In the wilderness there is,

(1.) Manna for them to eat, even Jesus Christ, to be fed on spiritually, John vi. 48—51, the only bread that can satisfy a soul. When the Egyptian provision is spent, the soul can no longer feed on the husks of the world, then the manna falls, the soul tastes the sweetness of Christ, in his person, offices, and benefits. It falls down about their tent-doors in the word of the everlasting gospel, exhibiting Christ with all his benefits to the soul; and it is gathered and ate by the application of saving faith, believing Christ to be offered, and taking Christ to itself, believing that it shall have life and salvation by him. And the more close, confident, and assured this application is, and the less mixed with doubting, the more the soul is fed.

(2.) Water out of the rock for them to drink, Exod. xvii. 6. This Rock is Christ, 1 Cor. x. 4. The Israelites might have perished in the wilderness for want of water, had it not been brought out of the rock; so had sinners perished, but that the blood of Christ was shed for their life. Behold Christ smitten by the law, before he could be drink to our souls.—Costly provision for the travellers! this is their provision till they come to Canaan's land.

3. Sometimes they are allowed a song in the weary land, for their comfort and recreation by the way, Psalm cxix. 54, "Thy statutes have been my songs in the house of my pilgrimage." We find Israel in the wilderness often complaining, groaning, and mourning; that is the ordinary in the wilderness-world; but seldom singing, that is reserved for the exercise in the promised land. Yet I find Israel singing in the wilderness three times.

(1.) At their entry into the wilderness, just after they came out from the Red Sea, Exod. xv. So young converts frequently have a parcel of pleasant days at their first setting off in the wilderness-journey, Hos. ii. 14. Religion is new to them; they are like men newly brought out of a dark dungeon, to whom the light has a double sweetness; and the Lord even so deals with them, as fathers with their children who are learning to go, holding out an apple to them, which they are not to expect when they are more confirmed; and further, it is even to fit them for the hardships which they are afterwards to meet with.

(2.) When they were far on in the wilderness, and had been long in it, they sang upon the occasion of God's giving them a well without their complaining, or so much as asking for it, Numb. xxi. 17, "Then Israel sang this song, Spring up, O well, sing ye unto it." Many a heavy day had gone over their head between that and the last song they had had, (I reckon not their song at the idolatry of the golden calf, Exod. xxxii. 18, which ended in sorrow.) The fiery serpents had been among them a little before. Yet God made them sing again. Thus sometimes God surprises the travellers with mercy after many a heavy day, that they think they will never sing more, and their souls have forgotten joy; yet he causes them to take down their harps from the willows, and puts a new song in their mouth; while he causes the wells of salvation to spring up to them.

(3.) In their last station in the wilderness, when they were encamping by Jordan, before they passed it, Deut. xxxi. 22, and chap. xxxii. It was forty years betwixt this and their first song. Thus they may have a weary time of it through the wilderness, who yet, when they come to the Jordan of death, shall be made to sing there the sweetest song that ever they sang, like the swan singing sweetest when a-dying. The nearer the rivers come to the sea, they are the sooner met by the tide. Motions in nature are so much the swifter as they come nearer the centre. And it may be a very cloudy day in which the sun shall shine brightest at its setting, Zech. xiv. 6, 7.

4. The Lord is their banner in the wilderness, and so they may be sure of victory, they shall be conquerors in the war, Exod. xvii. 15. Though they must fight, yet Christ the true Joshua is upon their head; he sits in heaven, who has the balance of victory in his hand; and he is their friend, and the cause is his own. Nay, they shall be more than conquerors. Israel was armed with the spoils of the Egyptian army, and Sihon and Og's lands they got possession of. Though the believer's battle with the world, the devil, and his own corruptions be sore; yet the spoils thereby gained are sweet, Psalm lxxiv. 14. They produce sweet experience of the Lord's goodness, Rom. v. 3, 4. Jacob was a man whose life had more trials than any of the Patriarchs; but as true as it was, it had more signal experiences too.

5. There is healing in the wilderness for them, for the wounds got there. There are fiery flying serpents to bite the people there, and they cannot miss the bites of the old serpent now and then. But there is the brazen serpent to look to and be healed; the ordinance relative thereto, we have, Numb. xxi. 8, 9, "And the Lord said unto

Moses, Make thee a fiery serpent, and set it upon a pole: and it shall come to pass, that every one that is bitten, when he looketh upon it, shall live. And Moses made a serpent of brass, and put it upon a pole; and it came to pass, that if a serpent had bitten any man, when he beheld the serpent of brass, he lived." This wilderness-world is the haunt of the old serpent, his prevailing temptations are his bites, the guilt remaining stings and galls the conscience; but Jesus Christ lifted up on the cross, and on the pole of the gospel, being looked to by faith, they are healed, Isa. xlv. 22. So Isa. xxxiii. *ult.*, "The inhabitant shall not say, I am sick: the people that dwell therein shall be forgiven their iniquity." And how often soever they be bitten, still the look of faith will be a healing look.

6. *Lastly.* We must not forget the tabernacle in the wilderness, which was the comfort of the godly Israelites there. There they had their stated meetings, and when anything more than ordinary ailed them in the wilderness, they used to draw towards the tabernacle. The tabernacle of gospel-ordinances is the great comfort of the travellers towards Zion. I shall only observe, that,

(1.) It was the place of meeting, namely, with God. The cloud of glory rested on it, and thence God spake. Gospel-ordinances are the place of meeting betwixt the Lord and his people in this wilderness-world, Prov. viii. 34, 35, and therefore they are even the pleasantest things in the wilderness.

(2.) It was coarse without, but rich and fine within. There was the golden candlestick, the shewbread table, incense-altar, ark, &c. All which believers have in Christ enjoyed in the ordinances.

(3.) *Lastly.* It was a moveable and slender thing. The tabernacle of gospel-ordinances is so. But wherever the Israelites went in the wilderness, they took the tabernacle with them. And the travellers to Zion, go where they will, dare not leave their religion, or their duties behind them. The tabernacle was often removed in the wilderness; but where it went, they went; none have a tack of the gospel; but wherever it goes, the travellers will go after it, cost what it will. Coarse fare and hard lodging with the gospel, will be by them preferred to the world's advantages without it. The tabernacle was suited to the wilderness, they had no temple there, that was reserved for the promised land of rest; but in heaven they shall have it, Rev. iii. 12.

I proceed now to the practical improvement of this subject.

USE I. Of information. From what is said we may draw the following inferences.

1. The people of God need not be surprised, that they meet with many hardships and trials in the world, and that it is a strange

world to them, John xvi. *ult.* While they are in it, they are in a wilderness. How then can they expect other than a wilderness-life? That the desert is to be turned into a paradise, nobody expects; why then look we to see the world other than a wilderness, if we mind for heaven? These things are useful.

(1.) To keep believers from sitting down in it, as their dwelling-place, Cant. iv. 8; or resting-place. A smiling world hugs many to death in its embraces; and the ease many find in it so charms the carnal heart, that the promised land is forgot, Matth. xvii. 4.

(2.) To quicken their pace out of it, and so work together for good to them, Rom. viii. 28. As a boisterous wind blowing on the back of the traveller, makes him sometimes run, while otherwise he would walk; so afflictions and trials put the believer to his duty, when he would not otherwise apply to it, and wean his heart more from the world; Micah vii. 7, "Therefore I will look unto the Lord; I will wait for the God of my salvation; my God will hear me."

(3.) To make heaven more desirable, 2 Cor. v. 4. The tossing they meet with on the sea of this world, makes them long for the shore, Job. vii. 2. And as rest is not so sweet to any as to the weary, nor meat as to the hungry; so heaven must be the more sweet in the enjoyment, that the believer has a weary life here.

2. They have good reason to bear all the hardships of their wilderness-lot patiently, and with Christian fortitude and cheerfulness. And that (1.) Because they will not last, they will be over ere long; they are going up from the wilderness. What inconveniencies are upon the road, the traveller matters not much, because he is not to stay with them. He may wonder indeed how people can dwell in a place to him so unpleasant; but it is but a light thing to him, because he is only a passenger. Indeed it is no wonder that the world's hardships be intolerable to them, who have no other portion but the things of the world; but they cannot be intolerable to the believer, who has a better portion, even one in heaven. (2.) Because the heavenly Canaan which the wilderness-road leads to, will make amends for all; "God shall then wipe away all tears from their eyes; and there shall be no more death, neither sorrow, nor crying, neither shall there be any more pain; for the former things are passed away," Rev. xxi. 4. Though the way be a rugged one, it leads to a paradise. Christ's espoused bride will forget all the wilderness-hardships, when she comes home to the marriage chamber in the Bridegroom's Father's house. (3.) Their lot is a wise mixture, take it at the worst. There are advantages allowed to balance the hardships, as ye have heard. There *is* no strait they can be in, in the wilderness, but there is help for it in the provision made for

them there. If the wilderness be a weary land, there are statutes that may be songs to them there, &c.

3. They are not Israelites indeed, nor espoused to Christ, who are not going up from this world as a wilderness, in heart and affection, in life and conversation. And such may lay their account, that their carcases will fall in the wilderness, and they shall not see Canaan's land. And such are,

(1.) Those whose hearts were never yet loosed from this world, and married to Christ, Matth. xiii. 44, 45. When man fell off from God, he fell to the creature, and his heart was wedded to it as the spring of his content and satisfaction. All the crosses in the world will not loose this knot; only efficacious grace discovering Christ in his surpassing glory to the sinner will do it.

(2.) Those who are walking according to the course of this world, Eph. ii. 2, framing their lives by worldly principles, being actuated by worldly motives, and acting for worldly ends as their chief design. Thus they are conformed to the world, which speaks them natives of the wilderness-world, not pilgrims in it. These, however their voice may be Jacob's, their hands are Esau's; though they pretend to be going heavenward, they are in the way to destruction.

The characters of them that walk are,

(1.) To do as the most do, not regarding how the best do; contrary to that plain injunction, Exod. xxiii. 2, "Thou shalt not follow a multitude to do evil." Thus the world is like a dunghill, where one part corrupts another, men fearlessly venturing on those courses and ways on which they see many before them. This is the downright reverse of going up from the wilderness, being a going along with the world, from which the apostle dehorts, Rom. xii. 2, "Be not conformed to this world."

(2.) To make the world one's business, and religion the by-hand work at best; not remembering what our Lord says, Matth. vi. 24, "No man can serve two masters; for either he will hate the one, and love the other; or else he will hold to the one, and despise the other. Ye cannot serve God and mammon." This is the way of the world, who look on their carnal interests as their chief interests, which therefore get the flower and strength of their affections. Whereas gracious souls go quite the contrary way, counting all things but loss, yea but dung that they may win Christ, Phil. iii. 8. And so our Lord directs us, Matth. vi. 33, to "seek first the kingdom of God, and his righteousness."

(3.) To step over conscience deliberately, to gratify lusts. Conscience among the men of the world is a very weak thing; and all its dictates, and the consideration of God's word as our rule, and

God's honour as concerned in men's actions, go very short way with them. Let the unjust man see gain within his reach, and the sensual man what may please his sensual lust; though God's command, honour, and conscience be between him and them, he can step over these, tread on them all, and gratify his lust, Hos. xii. 7, 8, and xiii. 6.

USE II. Of caution. While ye are in the wilderness, beware of wilderness sins and snares. And beware of,

1. Unbelief. That was a wilderness-sin of Israel's, Psalm. lxxviii. 22, "They believed not in God, and trusted not in his salvation." Yea, it was the sin that kept the whole generation that came out of Egypt, out of Canaan, Heb. iii. 18, 19. Many that seem to have been set fair on the way to the heavenly Canaan, come short of it this way. They believe not the record that God hath given concerning his Son, and so they never embrace Christ but perish. And the unbelief of saints while they are in the wilderness, does them much harm. It plucks away from their strength, and leaves them most unfit for their journey.

2. Murmuring, 1 Cor. x. 10. Many times God's anger was kindled against Israel for their murmurings in the wilderness. And it is incident to us in this wilderness-world, through the trials, crosses, and troubles that must be met with there. They had need of mortified affections that travel the wilderness-way, else they cannot in patience possess their souls. And when people have lost their patience, and their spirits are on the fret, everything ruffles them, and the hard way becomes harder.

3. Lusting, 1 Cor. x. 6. Let not the loose be given to your hearts, to fix on any thing which providence sees meet to withhold from you, so that ye must have it, and cannot be satisfied without it. Thus the Israelites lusted for flesh, and they got it with a vengeance, Numb. xi., Psalm lxxviii. 30, 31. And it is ordinary that what people pull off the tree of providence before it be ripe for them, sets their teeth on edge, and proves a snare to them. There is nothing better than a weaned heart to fit one for the wilderness-way.

4. Looking back to Egypt, Numb. xiv. 4. There is a root of apostacy in every one's heart, though broken in the sincere, yet reigning in others; hence it comes to pass, that many go far back, and lose what they have attained in religion, making themselves new work, with difficulty to recover what they threw away; and many fall away for good and all, and never recover. We had much need to take heed to the first rising of these evil motions in the heart; Psalm xlv. 10, "Hearken, O daughter, and consider, and incline thine ear; forget also thine own people, and thy father's house."

5. Fawning and flattering enemies, Numb. xxv. 17, 18. Pharaoh's

pursuit with his chariots and horses, Amalek's sword and bow, did not the mischief to Israel in the wilderness, that the daughters of Moab did, Numb. xxv. Balaam tried all his art to curse them, but could do them no harm by all his enchantments; but the Midianitish women ruined them with theirs, ver. 9. The church of God has often weathered out the storm of persecution, and came off victorious; while she has been ruined with the soft methods of the enemy. And many have stood out against the frowning world, that have been cast down with the smiling world. They have been drawn to destruction with silken cords of temptation, who could not be driven to it with iron rods.

6. *Lastly*. The mixed multitude, Exod. xii. 38. They were a black sight to Israel in the wilderness, a sad snare to them, Numb. xi. 4. They came in among them from a carnal principle of worldly interest, and were a snare to them, and their carcases fell in the wilderness. When God brings his church out of the house of bondage, and gives her peace, a company of carnal men driving their own worldly interest, join them like a swarm of insects in a summer-day, (Exod. xii. 38, a great mixture, Heb.); and the more their number increases, the more mischief they do to her true interests, sacrificing them to their own. It is not a little owing to the influence of that mixed multitude both of ministers and professors, that religion and its interests are at so low an ebb this day; and therefore we have ground to expect a stroke, come from what quarter it will, that will make a dispersion among us, and lessen our numbers, Ezek. xx. 37, 38. In the meantime beware of those who have a name to live, and are dead; formal professors often hurt a Christian more than the profane.

Use III. Of exhortation. And,

First, Ye who profess to be espoused to Christ, evidence the reality of it by your going up from the wilderness-world with him in heart and affection, in the progress of sanctification, and contempt of the world, holding off from the ways of it. To press this, I offer the following motives.

Mot. 1. Without this ye cannot evidence your sincerity, 1 John ii. 15. If your treasure be in heaven, your heart will be there. If Christ be indeed your espoused Husband, ye will forsake your father's house for him, and follow him. But many give him the hand and not the heart; and therefore though called by his name, dwell at their father's house still.

2. Without this ye will bring a reproach on religion, which suffers extremely by those who profess Christ, and yet follow the way of the world, Rom. ii. 24. Alas! for the wounds thus given to reli-

gion by the worldly disposition of the professors of it, whose untender lives, and covetous practices, proclaim them sons of earth.

3. *Lastly.* Ye may be very useful for Christ in the world this way, by commending religion practically at this rate to the consciences of carnal men. "Who is this that goeth up from the wilderness, leaning upon her Beloved?" say the daughters of Jerusalem. What can have more influence upon them, than to see men dead to the world, heavenly in their disposition, walking as pilgrims on the earth? It is a noble testimony for God.

(1.) To the vanity of the world, while men in their practice tread on that which carnal men set their hearts upon. What avails it for a man to talk of the world's vanity, while he is still griping it as his life, cannot part with it at God's call, for God's honour and service; but, on the contrary, is dishonouring God, and wounding his own soul, to gain it? That is building with the one hand, and destroying with the other.

(2.) To the reality and excellency of religion, and heavenly things, 1 Pet. iv. 4; Cant. iii. 6. It speaks a power in religion that can carry men above these perishing things, and that they must be fed from some other quarter, that so little value the streams of earthly things.

Secondly, Strangers to Christ, be espoused to him, that ye may go up with him from this wilderness-world, to his Father's house in the heavenly Canaan, believe that Christ is offered in an everlasting marriage-covenant to you. Embrace ye and accept, and so close with him as your head and husband, for time and eternity. I offer the following motives to enforce this exhortation.

MOTIVE I. Jesus Christ is really and truly in suit of your souls. This is the gospel-offer; Hos. ii. 19, "I will betroth thee unto me for ever, yea, I will betroth thee unto me in righteousness, and in judgment, and in loving-kindness, and in mercies;" and nothing will hinder but the want of your consent; Matth. xxii. 4, "All things are ready; come unto the marriage." He has with his precious blood bought a bride to himself, and he comes in the gospel to gain her heart to himself. And he is come to you this day; O then slight not the offer.

2. If ye accept of Christ, he will carry you up from this wilderness-world to his Father's house, where the marriage will be solemnised for ever. He will leave none of his behind him. There may be a time betwixt the espousals and marriage; but in that time he is carrying them to the marriage-chamber.

3. There is no loosing of the heart from the world without engaging it to Jesus Christ, Matth. xiii. 45, 46. It is the discovery of the

one pearl that makes one give over seeking the many. The heart of man is like a child that will not let the knife go out of its hand, till something that pleases it better is put into it. Though the devil go out, if the house be empty, he will return again, Matth. xii. 44, 45.

4. *Lastly,* If ye are not espoused to Christ, ye will fall in the wilderness, and never see the heavenly Canaan, Heb. iv. 12. They will have no access to the marriage above, that are not espoused to Christ here below. Nor will they be transplanted into the paradise above, who are not first planted in the nursery of grace below.

Thirdly. I invite, and sound an alarm to you all, to go up from this wilderness world with Christ. Rise, ye that are espoused to him, and come away. Rise, ye dwellers in the wilderness. Take him as your head and husband, and go along with him towards the heavenly Canaan, leaving this world in heart and affection.

QUEST. How shall I get up from the wilderness world, how will I get through it to the heavenly Canaan, while the journey is so hard and difficult for a poor weak creature? ANSW. I give you your directions and advice in a third doctrine from the text.

DOCTRINE. The way to get up from the wilderness-world to the heavenly Canaan, is to go all along leaning on Jesus Christ by faith. The way to live well in this world, till we come to heaven, is to live by faith.

Here I shall briefly shew what it is to go leaning, or to live by faith; and that we are allowed to go thus.

I. I shall shew briefly what it is to go leaning, or to live by faith.

1. It supposes the soul's taking, receiving, and embracing Christ for its head and husband, John i. 12. In the gospel Jesus Christ is offered, presented, and exhibited to every one that hears it, as the Father's gift to them, Isa. ix. 6; John iv. 10. He says in effect, "Poor souls, ye can never of yourselves make your way up through the wilderness; but I freely give you a strong one to lean upon. Take him and welcome." Hereupon the soul takes its hold of Christ for that end, the soul believes the gospel offer or promise as made to itself, saying in effect, "Then he is mine by the free offer made to me;" which implies the heart's consent to take him, and so the espousals are made, 1 John v. 11. It bears a going,

2. Cleaving to him, Acts xi. 23. Faith joins the soul to the Lord, so as to be one with him; and so holds the gripe, and will not quit it. The believer hangs by Christ, by the word of the gospel; and as the weak woman dares not lean to her own strength, but cleaves to her husband on the journey, so does the believer to Christ.

3. A going on under a sense of weakness, 2 Cor. iii. 5. There are two causes of one's going leaning upon another. One is love, the other weakness; both concur here. The believer loves Christ as his Lord and Husband, and therefore will lean on him; he is sensible of utter weakness and inability to make the journey in his own strength, and therefore must lean on him. Faith is a self-emptying grace, and therefore is chosen to be the mean of communication on our part betwixt the Lord and us, Rom. iv. 16.

4. A going on, laying our weight on the Lord Jesus for the whole of the journey, Psalm lv. 22. When the believer sets out with Christ, he says to him, "All thy wants be on me." "So be it," says the believing soul, and so rolls itself upon him for all. Hence faith is called a staying, Isa. l. 10, as an old man stays himself upon his staff; a believing on Christ, as a chief corner-stone, *i. e.* laying the weight on him, as the foundation, 1 Pet. ii. 6.

5. *Lastly.* A going on, with a persuasion that we shall be borne up and borne through by him, 2 Tim. i. 12. This is the plain import of leaning on Christ; for none will ever lean on that for help, concerning which they have no manner of persuasion that they shall be helped by it. Thus faith is called trusting in God, relying on him, both which bear this persuasion. And they that would remove this from the nature of faith, would destroy it, and leave us a mere wavering opinion in its stead.

But as one may lean trembling, so faith may be accompanied with doubting. But as trembling belongs not to the nature of leaning, but is opposite to it; so doubting belongs not to the nature of faith, but is opposite to it. And the more trembling the less leaning, so the more doubting the less faith.

This going up from the wilderness, leaning, is walking in Christ Jesus as we have received him, Col. ii. 6, which is the only true holiness competent to fallen man.

II. I shall shew, that we are allowed to go thus leaning. Consider, that,

1. The Father has appointed the Mediator for this very end, that so he may bring many sons to glory, Psalm lxxxix. 19, "I have laid help upon one that is mighty; I have exalted one chosen out of the people." The first man, with all his children in his loins, set off alone through the world, on his own stock; and fell, being unable to make the journey. Wherefore now the strength for all the heirs of glory is lodged in Christ, and they are allowed to live and lean on him; 1 Cor. i. 30, "But of him are ye in Christ Jesus, who of God is made unto us wisdom, and righteousness, and sanctification, and redemption." 2 Tim. ii. 1, "Thou therefore, my son, be strong in the grace that is in Christ Jesus."

2. We are called and commanded to lean on him; Psalm lv. 22, "Cast thy burden upon the Lord, and he shall sustain thee." Prov. iii. 5, 6, "Trust in the Lord with all thine heart; and lean not into thine own understanding. In all thy ways acknowledge him, and he shall direct thy paths." Psalm xxxvii. 5, "Commit thy way unto the Lord; trust also in him, and he shall bring it to pass." Isa. xxvi. 3, 4, "Thou wilt keep him in perfect peace, whose mind is stayed on thee; because he trusteth in thee. Trust ye in the Lord for ever: for in the Lord Jehovah is everlasting strength." It is the great duty called for in the Old and New Testament. We honour the Father and the Son, by doing this through the Spirit.

3. To pretend to go another way, is an abomination to the Lord, Prov. iii. 9. We know no holiness of Adam's fallen children, but what is a walking in Jesus Christ. Men may call the obedience given to the law otherwise, holiness; but a holy God will never own it as such, when it savours not of union with his Son.

Use. Then if ye would go up from the wilderness of this world to the heavenly Canaan, go leaning on Jesus Christ.

1. Go leaning on him for light to know your duty, Prov. iii. 5. Ye are in the wilderness; let him be eyes to you there; look to him, as the Israelites did to the motions of the cloud, for your direction. He is the great Prophet and Teacher; close your own eyes that ye may be guided by his word and Spirit.

2. Go leaning on him for strength to perform your duty, Phil. iv. 13. It will not be your weak hands that will work the work, nor your feeble knees that will perform the journey. The strength must come from him who is the Head. And ye must go on borrowed legs.

3. *Lastly.* Go leaning on him for acceptance, and the happy issue of your journey, Eph. i. 6. It is through him alone that any step in the Lord's way can be accepted, and by him alone we can be brought into the eternal rest.

In all this ye are to believe the word of promise, and on the credit of it to set about your duty, renouncing yourselves, and believing and applying the sufficiency treasured up in Christ.

Great is your need of leaning; ye have great work to do, a great journey to go, much weakness hangs about you, much opposition ye must encounter; yet forward ye must be out of the wilderness to the heavenly Canaan, else ye perish.

ENOCH'S CHARACTER AND TRANSLATION EXPLAINED; WITH A DESCRIPTION OF WALKING WITH GO , AS THAT IN WHICH THE LIFE OF RELIGION LIES.*

GENESIS v. 24,

And Enoch walked with God, and he was not; for God took him.

IT is too evident, that the generation we live in is in a declining condition; that professors are few, but real Christians fewer by far. Religion with many is turned to be the object of their ridicule; and among those that own it, to merely dry and sapless notions, for the most part. Few now are added to the church, or brought over out of the devil's camp. True godliness languishes, and serious experimental religion wears out. Therefore I would press religion in the life and power of it, on those that would save themselves from this untoward generation.

Here shines the brightest star in the patriarchal age, which having given light to the lower world for a time, was afterwards translated into a higher sphere, and passed out of the world in as un usual a manner as he lived in it. For as men live in the world, so ordinarily they go out of it.

There is a long account here, where nothing is marked but names and numbers, men's living and dying, till we come to Enoch, whose singular piety is recorded. OBSERVE. The life of man is for the most part a vain thing, of which, by the sleeping of some, and the slumbering of others, nothing remains remarkable, but that they lived and died. But close walking with God serves another and better purpose, than to cause one just fill up room in the world for a while.

From the short history of these antediluvian patriarchs, we may learn one lesson, that will serve us all our days, viz. That we must die, how long soever we live. It is reported of one, that by hearing this chapter read in the church, he got such an impression of his own death, that he turned religious, that he might die well. *Drexel. de œtern.*

But from the history of Enoch we may learn two lessons. 1. How to live well in this world. 2. The happiness that abides those in another world, who so live here; even eternal happiness of soul and body with the Lord.

* Several sermons preached at Ettrick, in the year 1716.

In the words there is remarked a real preaching that was given to the old world by Enoch ; a life-preaching ; for his conversation preached to them, what religion was, and what was their great duty, viz. walking with God ; a removal-preaching, (we cannot say his death preached, for he did not die ; but his passage out of this world preached), that there is another and a better life with God in another world, both for soul and body. And this is no doubt marked, to shew us the mercy bestowed on that generation, that the godly in it might be encouraged, and the wicked left without excuse, while such a bright star shone so fair in that dark age. For it is observable, that his walking with God is twice told, once, ver. 22, and here again in the text, in conjunction with his happy removal, giving us a compendious body of divinity, written for the use of that age especially, (not excluding others), in this man's life and translation out of the world. So that God left not himself without a witness in that degenerate age. They not only heard, but saw in him, the power of godliness, and the reward of it too.

OBSERVE, Men will not only have the best instructions and warnings they get from the world, but those they get from the examples of holy men, to answer for in the day of accounts. There are silent preachers, who yet speak home, as Noah, who " being warned of God of things not seen as yet, moved with fear, prepared an ark to the saving of his house ; by the which he condemned the world ;" Heb. xi. 7 ; and the men of Nineveh, and the queen of the south, of whom our Lord says, Matth. xii. 41, 42, " The men of Nineveh shall rise in judgment with this generation, and shall condemn it, because they repented at the preaching of Jonas, and behold, a greater than Jonas is here. The queen of the south shall rise up in the judgment with this generation, and shall condemn it ; for she came from the uttermost parts of the earth to hear the wisdom of Solomon, and behold, a greater than Solomon is here." Examples of a holy life, if they do not lead spectators to heaven, will drive them more deeply into destruction.

Though it is charitably thought, that all the patriarchs were good men, yet surely the age wherein Enoch lived was a very degenerate and profane age, Methuselah his son died the same year the deluge came on. He lived nine hundred and sixty-nine years. Enoch walked with God three hundred years. So from his translation there were six hundred and sixty-nine to the deluge. Of that they got one hundred and twenty years' warning of the deluge ; so that to that time there were but five hundred and forty-nine years. There were none of those here mentioned but they lived more than seven hundred years. And God's Spirit had been long striving with the generation before the last hundred and twenty years. So that we may well reckon that many of those who lived in Enoch's days, were of those God's Spirit had so long striven with, and that were swept away by the deluge; and consequently that it was a very degenerate and profane age he lived in, wherein men had come the length to talk and act boldly against the God that made them, as appears from Jude 14, 15, "Enoch also, the seventh from Adam, prophesied of these, saying, Behold, the Lord cometh with ten thousands of his saints, to execute judgment upon all, and to convince all that are ungodly among them, of all their ungodly deeds which they have ungodly committed, and of all their hard speeches which ungodly sinners have spoken against him."

OBSERVE, Be the times never so bad, it is men's own fault they are bad too. Eminent holiness, and intimate communion with God, may be attained in the worst of times. While that generation was running to ruin, Enoch walked with God.

The reasons are,

1. Because however men grow worse and worse, heaven is still as good and bountiful as ever; Isa. lix. 1, 2, "Behold, the Lord's hand is not shortened, that it cannot save; neither his ear heavy that it cannot hear, but your iniquities have separated between you and your God, and your sins have hid his face from you, that he will not hear." God's door still stands open, though the generation conspire to trouble it very little for supply. Our Lord will never shut his door upon his people, because they are few; but it shall stand open as long as there is one that hath business in his house; Micah ii. 7, "O thou that art named the house of Jacob, is the Spirit of the Lord straitened? are these his doings? do not my words do good to him that walketh uprightly?"

2. Because those that mind for heaven, must row against the stream always; and if they do not, they will be called down the stream in the best of times; for, says our Lord, Matth. xi. 12, "From the days of John the Baptist, until now, the kingdom of heaven suffereth violence, and the violent take it by force." If people will ply the throne of grace, and resolutely set themselves against the epidemical disease of their day, they may keep lively in the midst of a dead crew, though with much difficulty, as our Lord observes; Rev. iii. 4, "Thou hast a few names even in Sardis, which have not defiled their garments."

3. The badness of the times affords matter to excite God's people the more to their duty, and close walking with God. The profaneness and formality of those they live among, and the dishonour done to God thereby, should be like oil to the flame of their holy love and

zeal, as it was to David; Psalm cxix. 126, 127, "It is time for thee, Lord, to work, for they have made void thy law. Therefore I love thy commandments above gold, yea, above fine gold." The prospect of what must needs be the issue of such apostasy of a generation may also quicken them; even as one is the more concerned to see to his own safety, that the rest of the family are pulling down the house about their own ears; as was the case with Noah, who, among a very wicked and abandoned people, had this character, "Noah was a just man and perfect in his generations, and Noah walked with God," Gen. vi. 9.

4. *Lastly*. Because as the Lord shews himself most concerned for the welfare of those who are most concerned for his honour; so the worse the times are, they that cleave to him closely may expect to fare the better, as Noah also did, when the Lord said to him, "Come thou, and all thy house into the ark: for thee have I seen righteous before me in this generation," Gen. vii. 1. Moses never had a more glorious manifestation of God, than at the time when the Israelites had fallen into the idolatry of the golden calf, and God was about to destroy the whole nation; as you will find by comparing Exod. xxxii. 10, and chap. xxxiii. and xxxiv.

Use 1. Learn that those who keep not up communion with God, in the life and power of religion, in evil times, are in God's account joined and embarked with the generation of his wrath; and be who they will, they will smart with the rest for it, though they put not forth their hands to the notorious abominations of the times they live in. Hence is that threatening, Zeph. i. 12, "It shall come to pass at that time, that I will search Jerusalem with candles, and punish the men that are settled on their lees; that say in their heart, The Lord will not do good, neither will he do evil." It is a heavy word that sets formal hypocrites and profane wretches on one and the same bottom; Psalm cxxv. *ult.*, "As for such as turn aside unto their crooked ways, the Lord shall lead them forth with the workers of iniquity."

2. Bad example with its influence will not excuse people before the Lord. While it is no comfort to go to hell with company, there can be no safety in following a multitude to do evil. What! will men think that because the conspiracy against God and holiness is strong, therefore they may join in it; that because serious godliness is going over the brae, therefore they may give it a push? But wo will be to them that give an unhallowed touch to God's wain when it is at the halting.

3. To be complaining of the evil of the times, sighing and going backward in religion, is a fruitless unavailing complaint, neither

pleasing to God, nor profitable to one's self. For at no time does religion consist in talking, but in walking with God. And that is but to condemn ourselves out of our own mouths.

4. *Lastly*. Let us be exhorted to study the power and reality of religion in these dregs of time. Let us draw the nearer to God, that we see so many going far from him. And as we would not bring the wrath of God on ourselves, let us neither join with a profane generation, nor continue on our lees with a formal dead-hearted generation, strangers to the power of godliness. Consider here,

1. Enoch's holy life in this world.
2. His happy removal into a better world.

FIRST, Let us consider Enoch's holy life in this world; "Enoch walked with God." The Spirit of God puts a special remark on this. It is Enoch's honour, that he did not walk as others did, after their lusts. Yea, he walked more holily and closely with God, than other good men of that age.

OBSERVE 1. God takes special notice of those who are best when others are worst, Gen. vi. 9. We see this in the instance of Noah in the old world, and of Lot in Sodom; likewise of those mentioned Ezek. ix. 4, concerning whom the Lord said, "Go through the midst of the city, through the midst of Jerusalem, and set a mark upon the foreheads of the men that sigh, and that cry for all the abominations that be done in the midst thereof;" and those taken notice of Mal. iii. 16, 17, "Then they that feared the Lord, spake often one to another, and the Lord hearkened, and heard it, and a book of remembrance was written before him for them that feared the Lord, and that thought upon his name. And they shall be mine, saith the Lord of hosts, in that day when I make up my jewels, and I will spare them as a man spareth his own son that serveth him."

1. To be thus argues an ingenuous spirit, a love to the Lord for himself, and a love to his way for its likeness to himself; that the soul is carried thus to it against the stream of the corruption of the age.

2. It argues not only grace, but the strength of grace. It must be strong faith, love, &c. that so much bear out against the strong temptation to apostasy, arising from the combination of a generation against God and his way. To be holy when the helps to a holy life are least in the world, argues the vigour of grace in the heart.

USE. Labour ye then to be best while others are worst, to confront the impiety of the generation wherein ye live. Do they indulge themselves in licentiousness? be ye the more strict and holy in your walk. Do they take up with mere externals in religion? strive ye the rather to get into the inner court, to taste and see, and here to have communion with God.

OBSERVE. 2. It is the honour of a professor of religion, to outgo others in the matter of close walking with God. God himself is glorious in holiness. The more holy one is, the more like is he to God. The liker he is to God, the more honourable is he.

USE 1. This lets us see what would be a blessed emulation among professors, viz. that we were striving who should be most tender, holy, and circumspect. O that that were brought in, in the room of all our strifes and contests about practices and opinions, which eat out the life of religion in our day! But alas! real holiness is little regarded, and therefore little striven for.

2. It must be a godless-like mark in any person, to have the serpentine grudge rise in their breasts against others, as they see them eminent for holy and tender walking. These are the persons most beloved and honoured of God; and it looks devilish-like to hate them, and have one's heart rise against them, for that very reason for which God loves them.

In the first part of the words we have,

1. The person characterized; and that is Enoch. There was another of this name descended from Cain, who had a city called after his name; Gen. iv. 17. Immortality is desired of all; and because men cannot stave off death, they follow after a shadow of immortality, that at least their name may live when they are gone. Therefore that has been an ancient custom, for men to call their lands after their own names; Psalm xlix. 11. How much better was it with this Enoch, that took that course to get on him the name of the city of God, which Christ promises to write on all his people? Rev. iii. 12. The city called by the name of the other Enoch was destroyed by the deluge, and is now unknown; but the city of God lasts still, and will last for ever.

OBSERVE. True piety is the best way to honour, even to true honour. For "the righteous shall be in everlasting remembrance," when "the memory of the wicked shall rot."

Enoch signifies dedicated, initiated, instructed. His life answered his name, for he lived as one devoted to the Lord. OBSERVE. It is the duty of those devoted to God by their godly parents, to devote themselves to the Lord. And where grace comes in with good education, it ordinarily makes men famous in their generation, and signally serviceable to God.

He was the seventh from Adam, and a prophet, who foretold the last judgment, even in that early age of the church; Jude 14, above cited. He was like Noah, a preacher of righteousness in his day; and like John Baptist, a burning and shining light, burning in his conversation, shining in his doctrine.

OBSERVE. They that live near God, are most likely to be put upon his secrets, and to know most of his mind; Psalm xxv. 14, "The secret of the Lord is with them that fear him; and he will shew them his covenant."

2. His character; he "walked with God." He lived like a man of another world; a life of close communion with God. It imports, (1.) That he was really religious; not only religious before men, but before God. OBSERVE. Religion lies inwardly. We are that really which we are before the Lord; Rom. ii. *ult.*, " He is a Jew which is one inwardly." (2.) He was eminently religious. OBSERVE. Men may attain to eminency in religion, in very bad times, by setting the Lord always before them. See here,

1*st*, What he was; a spiritual traveller through the world; he "walked." Whereas it is said of others, they "lived;" it is said of Enoch, "He walked with God." He looked on himself as a pilgrim and stranger in this present world; Heb. xi. 13, compare ver. 5, and did not sit down in it to take up his abode on this side Jordan.

OBSERVE. They that would live a life of communion with God, must live as pilgrims in this world, as travellers through it to a better country.

1. Their hearts must be loosed from the world, bidding an eternal farewell to it as a portion; 1 John ii. 15. The heart gone from God naturally sits down on the creature, to suck the sap of it, and to pursue it as its chief good. Now, the first step to the soul's thriving, is to lift the heart from the creature, and once fairly to give up with the vain world.

2. They must be fixed on the better country; Heb. xi. 14. They must look to the land that is afar off, resolutely aiming to be there, and therefore habitually keeping it in their eye, as the mark they desire to hit; Phil. iii. 20. Thus we shall be heavenly in the frame and disposition of our spirits.

3. They must keep death much in their view, the passage out of this world into the other; Job xiv. 14, "If a man die, shall he live again? all the days of my appointed time will I wait till my change come." See what a familiarity he had contracted with it; chap. xvii. 14, "I have said to corruption, Thou art my father; to the worm, Thou art my mother and my sister." This is the way to wean our hearts from the world, and to stir us up to converse much with another world.

4. *Lastly*. They must beware of dipping deep in things of this life, but go through the world lightly, like travellers, who serve themselves with a passing view of those parts they go through;

1 Cor. vii. 29—31, "But this I say, brethren, the time is short. It remaineth, that both they that have wives, be as though they had none; and they that weep, as though they wept not; and they that rejoice, as though they rejoiced not; and they that buy, as though they possessed not; and they that use this world, as not abusing it; for the fashion of this world passeth away."

The reason is, because the world is one of the great make-bates betwixt God and a soul. And so far as it gets in betwixt God and us, it causes an eclipse of the light of the Lord's countenance.

USE. As ever ye would live a life of communion with God, live as pilgrims in this world. The manna never fell from heaven in the wilderness, till the provision brought from Egypt was spent and done. Deny yourselves to this world, if ye would have the taste of things of a better world. When the vessels of your hearts are emptied of the love of the world, the oil of grace will run.

2*dly*, The company he kept while he was in the way; "He walked with God." He did not walk with the generation he lived in; did not go on with the multitude, thinking it enough to do as they did; but he "walked with God," being a follower of the Lord, keeping his eye on him.

OBSERVE. True religion makes one give up with the way of the world, and set God before them for all. It is the way of strangers from God to follow the course of this world; Eph. ii. 2. They that mind for heaven, must be nonconformists to the world; Rom. xii. 2. They must be practical separatists from the world, in life and conversation; Psalm xii. 7, as it was with Joshua, who said, chap. xxiv. 15, "As for me and my house, we will serve the Lord."

USE 1. See here what a graceless-like thing it is for people to content themselves to be like neighbour and others. Ah, Sirs, though all the world should approve you, if God condemn you, what will it avail? They that pin their faith or holiness on other people's sleeve, have neither faith nor holiness, and will never see heaven.

2. See the necessity of a religion beyond the reach of the common gang of the world; Zech. iii. 8. Ye must not satisfy yourselves with the religion that most part do; but press forward to leave them behind you, because they do not walk with God.

3*dly*, His constancy in the way of the Lord; he "walked incessantly" as the word signifies. He did not take his religion by fits and starts, as many do, but he kept a constant course of it. Ver. 22 tells us, he walked with God three hundred years, all the time he lived after he begat Methuselah. Though perhaps he was a good man while he lived single in his young days, yet his last days were his best days. His greatest eminency for piety was in the days of his married life; while his family was increasing, his soul was increasing too.

OBSERVE. A married state is a state of life very consistent with the soul's flourishing in religion.

USE. How unreasonable, then, is that excuse, which goes mighty far with the world; Luke xiv. 20, "I have married a wife, and therefore I cannot come?" It was not so with Enoch; the comforts of it did not so bewitch him, nor the cares of it so rack his spirit, but that he was one of the holiest and heavenliest men that ever lived. What a pity is it, that that state should be a state of declining in religion to so many, and that as their family increases, their soul's case goes to wreck? So that of their marriage-day it may be said, as John vi. 66, "From that time many of his disciples went back, and walked no more with him." It is a holy state, and a helpful one, by God's appointment. It must needs be a dreadful business, where the one proves a snare to the other, for apostasy from the life of God.

Secondly, There is Enoch's happy removal into a better world.

1. Consider his leaving of this world; "He was not:" no more in this world. Of all the rest it is said, they "died;" but of him only, "he was not," for he died not, but got out of the world without dying. He was taken off,

1st, Soon, being only three hundred and sixty-five years of age. That was in the midst of his days; for there were none of the patriarchs before the flood, but lived more than as long again.

OBSERVE. God ofttimes takes them soonest out of the world that are dearest to him. Why then should we be fond of long life? He was a man that was dear to God, and useful for God. And if he did not live long, he lived fast, and did more in his few days, than others in double the time. He had no loss, for the remainder of his days he got in heaven.

2dly, Suddenly; so the phrase seems to import; Psalm xxxvii. 36, and so the nature of the thing requires it to be; as in the case of Elijah; 2 Kings ii. 11, and those who shall be changed; 1 Cor. xv. 51, 52, cases parallel to this. He evanished.

OBSERVE. A sudden removal out of the world may befal the best of God's children. Why should the Lord's people then be afraid of sudden death? It does but make sore work short work; and they that are in Christ can never be taken habitually at least unprepared; and they that always walk habitually with God, are always actually prepared. Good old Eli died such a death.

2. Consider his transportation to heaven; "God took him;" took him home, took him up soul and body at once to himself into hea-

ven; Heb. xi. 5. God made a change on his corruptible body without death, even such a change as will be made on the bodies of the saints that shall be alive at Christ's second coming. So there was as great a difference betwixt his removal and that of others, as betwixt his life and theirs.

OBSERVE. When the saints leave the world, God takes them home to himself.

All the patriarchs mentioned in this chapter were alive at Enoch's translation, except Adam, who died some time before, and Noah, who was born some time after. Adam himself had heard the voice of God, and Noah got an eminent confirmation of his faith in his preservation in the ark. Enoch's translation might be confirming to the rest, in the faith of a future happy state of the saints, both in soul and body. And it was a sure pledge of the resurrection, that was then far off, and not yet come.

OBSERVE. The weight of the doctrine of the resurrection of the dead, which God so early confirmed. It is worthy to be remarked, how Enoch's body was carried to heaven before the law, Elijah's under the law, and Christ's under the gospel. So that each of the three great periods of the world's age had in it a notable pledge of the resurrection of the body.

USE. Let us then live and die in the faith of it; and while we live, live as those that look for it.

Having thus given a large practical explication of the text, I proceeed to observe a point of doctrine from them, as the ground of some further discourse.

DOCTRINE. The life of religion lies in walking with God; or, the great thing we should aim at for practical godliness, is to walk with God.

Here I shall,

I. Explain this walking with God.

II. Confirm the doctrine, that the life of religion lies in walking with God.

III. *Lastly.* Apply.

I. For explication of this walking with God, I shall consider it,

1. In the foundation thereof, with respect to our state.
2. In the matter of it, in respect of our frame and conversation.
3. In the properties thereof.

FIRST. I am to consider walking with God in the foundation thereof, with respect to our state. And so it pre-supposes,

First, Spiritual life restored to the soul in regeneration. Men are naturally dead to God and holiness; Eph. ii. 1, " dead in trespasses and sins." A dead man cannot walk, and a dead soul cannot walk with God. Before Lazarus once in his grave could move again, he behoved to be quickened and raised again. No wonder that many cannot walk with God, seeing they are strangers to the life of God. They live as they were born in a natural state. Consider,

1. The eye of the understanding is out, and man naturally is blind; Eph. v. 8. Walking with God is a regular walk; how then can the blind soul walk so? To walk at random is to walk contrary to God; Lev. xxvi. 21. *Heb.* Never a soul will stumble on the way of God; for while in the state of blindness, Satan and lusts lead the soul. Therefore we must be cured by divine illumination; and for this cause the gospel is preached; Acts xxvi. 18, "to open men's eyes, and to turn them from darkness to light."

2. The feet of the soul, the will and affections, are quite indisposed for walking with God, and they must be cured. Hence is the promise, Ezek. xxxvi. 26, 27, "A new heart will I give you, and a new spirit will I put within you, and I will take away the stony heart out of your flesh, and I will give you an heart of flesh. And I will put my Spirit within you, and cause you to walk in my statutes, and ye shall keep my judgments, and do them."

(1.) They are distorted, disjointed, and cannot ply to the way of God; Jer. xiii. 23, "Can the Ethiopian change his skin, or the leopard his spots? then may ye also do good, that are accustomed to do evil." They have got a set to backsliding from the Lord, and they cannot be cured without a miracle of grace. That must give them a new set, or we are undone for ever; Psalm lxxxv. ult., "Righteousness shall go before him; and shall set us in the way of his steps."

(2.) They are weak, and unable to bear us in his way, Rom. v. 6. We lost our strength in the loins of our first parents, and never recover it till we be in Christ, to partake of his Spirit. If the soul aim to rise, it cannot; if to walk, the legs fail under us. Nay,

(3.) They are powerless, John xv. 5, and vi. 44. There is power in them to carry us still further out of God's way, but they are absolutely unable to move heavenward, till they be endowed with power from on high. Therefore we are to be concerned for the new nature, the principle of spiritual life.

Secondly, Faith in God through Jesus Christ. We must come to God before we can walk with him, it is by faith we come to him, Heb. xi. 6. We are naturally at a distance from God; in the everlasting covenant God offers to meet us in Christ. So by coming to Christ we meet with God, that we may set off in our way with him. Whoso would walk with God,

1. Must take God for their God in the covenant, Heb. viii. 10, renouncing all others for him, and accepting him as their God and portion, to walk with him as their covenanted God. The world bears great bulk in sinners' eyes naturally, but we must look over it and above it, to the God that made it, that we may take up our souls' everlasting rest in him. So did Enoch, while the rest were following vanities; he closed his eyes on them, and came to God as his soul's home.

2. They must embrace Christ in the offer of the gospel, seeing in him only we can meet with God. God out of Christ is a consuming fire; but vailed with the flesh of Christ, he is a refreshing sun. We cannot walk with an absolute God, more than dry fuel can lie before a consuming fire.

Thirdly. A state of reconciliation with God; Amos iii. 3, "Can two walk together, except they be agreed?" Man naturally is in a state of enmity with God. And while that lasts, he can never walk with God dutifully to him, nor comfortably to himself. For in that state what we do can never be acceptable to God, nor can we look for comfort to ourselves by it; and hence Eliphaz advises, Job xxii. 21, "Acquaint now thyself with him, and be at peace; thereby good shall come unto thee." Therefore we must be in a justified state, having our sins pardoned for the sake of Christ, and so in a state of peace through the great Peace-maker. When God and a sinner in a state of enmity meet, what can be expected but,

1. Angry looks? No wonder he turn his back on such; so that though they come to Jerusalem, they see not the King's face; Hos. v. 6, "They shall go—to seek the Lord; but they shall not find him, he hath withdrawn himself from them."

2. Angry words? God can speak so as to make the conscience hear, where there is no audible voice; Psalm l. 16, "But unto the wicked God saith, What hast thou to do to declare my statutes, or that thou shouldst take my covenant in thy mouth?" That is a question that imports anger, upbraiding, accusing, and grief for the contempt put upon him. And O what a sad matter is it to have him angry with us in whose favour life lies; him to upbraid us, who does us all the good we get; him our accuser, who is our only intercessor; and him to be grieved with us, who only can make us glad?

3. Angry strokes? When enemies meet, no wonder there be blows a-dealing. Sometimes there are strokes on the body, 1 Cor. x. 1—6; strokes on the soul, Mal. i. *ult.* See how it was with the Israelites in the wilderness; Psalm cvi. 15, "He gave them their request, but sent leanness into their soul." Wherefore let us labour to have God for our friend in Christ, that we may walk with him.

Fourthly, Conversion, or turning to God. We are naturally turned away from God, and therefore are called to return to him, Hos. xiv. 1. Our hearts are turned away from himself; our feet are turned away from his way. We must turn back again ere we can walk with him.

1. Our hearts must be brought off the world to God; Cant. iv. 8, "Come with me from Lebanon, my spouse, with me from Lebanon: look from the top of Amana, from the top of Shenir and Hermon, from the lions' dens, from the mountains of the leopards." The first removing of the heart was from God to the creature, from the fountain to the muddy streams and broken cisterns, Jer. ii. 13. There men naturally seek their happiness, comfort, and satisfaction. But it must remove again, leave the bulky vanity, the fair deceitful nothing, and return to God. Our hearts must be lifted, our love, joy, delight, &c., off the creature, and set on God.

2. Our hearts must be brought from our lusts to the Lord, from our sins to our Saviour; we must say, "That which I see not, teach thou me; if I have done iniquity, I will do no more," Job xxxiv. 32. That day the soul returns to the Lord, the idols will be cast to the bats and to the moles, Isa. ii. 20. For if God get the throne in the heart, they will get the cross. It was in this case God observed Ephraim, and was well pleased with him; Jer. xxxi. 18—20, "I have surely heard Ephraim bemoaning himself thus, Thou hast chastised me, and I was chastised, as a bullock unaccustomed to the yoke; turn thou me, and I shall be turned, for thou art the Lord my God. Surely after that I was turned, I repented; and after that I was instructed, I smote upon my thigh; I was ashamed, yea, even confounded, because I did bear the reproach of my youth. Is Ephraim my dear son? is he a pleasant child? for since I spake against him I do earnestly remember him still, therefore my bowels are troubled for him; I will surely have mercy upon him, saith the Lord."

3. We must be brought out of ourselves unto God; Matthew xvi. 24, "If any man will come after me, let him deny himself." Man turning off from God turned into himself, and made himself his chief end, acting from himself and to himself. So we are naturally hemmed in within the cursed circle of self, out of which we must be turned ere we can walk with God. And,

(1.) Out of our self-wisdom, put in the room of Christ as a prophet. For thus saith God to all that would walk with him, "I will instruct thee, and teach thee in the way which thou shalt go; I will guide thee with mine eye," Psalm xxxii. 8. Whoso would give up themselves to the Lord, must, as it were, put out their own eyes, resolving never more to guide themselves, that they may follow the Lord, as Abraham did, Heb. xi. 8, who, at God's call, went out, not knowing whither he went.

(2.) Out of our self-righteousness, put in the room of Christ as a priest. We must come up to duties, and then come over them, renouncing all confidence in them, laying no weight on them in the point of commending us to the favour of God. For what stress is laid on them that way, derogates from the honour of him on whom the Father has laid help, and is inconsistent with the character of the true circumcision, Phil. iii. 3. Otherwise we cannot walk with God in duties.

(3.) Out of our self-will and self-ability, put in the room of Christ as a king. Man is naturally wilful, and will have his own liking, and do what seems good in his own eyes. But in the day that one comes to walk with God, he gives up with his own will, saying, " Thy will be done on earth, as it is in heaven." He gives it to be led as a captive after Christ's chariot wheels, so that he may draw it and drive over it, as seems good in his eyes, 2 Cor. x. 5.

Man also naturally goes into himself for strength wherewith to do commanded duty, being ignorant of Christ as the head of influences for sanctification. But in the day one comes to walk with God, he renounces his own stock as insufficient, and gives up himself to live by Christ, in the way of being daily supplied, John vi. 57. For then he sees the truth of that saying, " He that trusteth in his own heart is a fool; but whoso walketh wisely, he shall be delivered," Prov. xxviii. 26.

SECONDLY, I shall consider walking with God in the matter of it, in respect of our frame and conversation. And indeed this duty goes as broad as the whole law. I must take it up in some particulars. If we would have the life of religion in our walk, we must not walk at random.

First, We must walk with God in the way of habitual eyeing of him in all things. It is the neck-break of many, that God is not in all their thoughts, and the ruin of religion among professors, that they forget God, though he is not far from any of us. The heart is like a common inn, so thronged with strangers, that the master is not noticed, but thrust out to make room for others. It was otherwise with David; Psalm xvi. 1, " I have set the Lord always before me; because he is at my right hand, I shall not be moved."

1. We must eye him as our witness in all things. Let us say everywhere as Hagar, Gen. xvi. 13, " Thou God seest me," Let us fix on our hearts awful apprehensions of his omniscience and omnipresence, as Psalm cxxxix. 7, " Whither shall I go from thy spirit, or whither shall I flee from thy presence ?" There is a root of Atheism in our hearts that says, " The Lord hath forsaken the earth, and the Lord seeth not," Ezek. ix. 9. And O how ready are the best to forget,

though they are ever under the chalk of his eye, that he is a witness to every thought, word, and action! Thus walking with God implies,

(1.) The believing of his all-seeing eye, embracing it with a firm faith, that he is intimately acquainted with all our ways, Heb. iv. 13. His eye is on us where no other eye can see us, yea, where our own eyes cannot reach, that is, into our hearts. And where the true faith of this is, it will not want an impression of proportionable depth with the strength of the faith wherewith it is apprehended.

(2.) An habitual minding of this all-seeing eye that is on us, Psalm xvi. 8. Walkers with God are frequently sisting themselves in the presence of this God; and especially when the temptation comes, they look to him that sees them, and say, "Shall I do this great wickedness, and sin against God?"

(3.) A suitable respect to this all-seeing eye, influencing our hearts, lips, and lives, to beware of sin, and to be diligent and upright in duty. The eyes of a child will restrain people sometimes; how much more should the eye of God that is never off us?

2. Eye him as our Judge, to whom at length we must give an account, Rom. xiv. 10. Let us remember and often have in our mind, that word which at length will reach our ears, "Rise ye dead, and come to judgment." We might walk as we list, if we were never to be called to account. But there is not a thought, word, or action, but what must be judged, Rom. ii. 16; Eccl. xii. *ult.* We can never say there is more than a step betwixt us and the judgment-seat, and therefore there is good reason we should walk as prisoners going to the bar.

(1.) Let us walk as under the eye of an infinitely holy Judge, who cannot look on sin but with abhorrence, Hab. i. 13. He can never be brought by any means to approve of sin, how little soever we think of it. The least spot is offensive to the eyes of his jealousy, and he cannot away with it.

(2.) Let us walk as under the eye of an accurate Judge, from whom no crime can be hid, whose eyes no pretences nor fair colours can deceive. Let us remember when we come there, our crimes cannot be hid for want of evidence; for the omniscient Judge himself is witness to all, and that omniscience will pierce through all the vails wherewith we now cloke our sins.

(3.) Let us walk as under the eye of an impartial Judge. He is one that cannot be biassed either by feud or favour. He is no respector of persons, but rewards every one according to his work. The belief of this would make us impartial in our own cause; and if we were walking with God, we would sist our own cause without partiality.

3. Eye him as our Redeemer and Saviour; Isa. xlv. 22, "Look unto me, and be ye saved, all the ends of the earth: for I am God, and there is none else." To eye God as our witness and judge, without eyeing him as a God in Christ, atoned by his blood, would fright us away from him, so as we could never walk with him more. But that a guilty creature may walk with God, let him,

(1.) Eye the mercy of God in a Mediator; Isa. lv. 7, "Let the wicked forsake his way, and the unrighteous man his thoughts: and let him return unto the Lord, and he will have mercy upon him, and to our God, for he will abundantly pardon." That is a large covering under which may be hid all the guilt of our walk. It reaches deep and extends very far, Psalm lxxxvi. 13, "Great is thy mercy toward me: and thou hast delivered my soul from the lowest hell." In our most accurate walking, and when we have done our utmost, there will be need of grace and mercy. And we must believingly apply to it, that when we have fallen, we may rise up again and walk.

(2.) Eye the righteousness of a Redeemer. Had the most close walker with God nothing to look to but the righteousness of his own works, he would never have ground of joy all the way through the wilderness. But the naughtiness of his own righteousness makes him look often to the imputed righteousness, and there he joys; Isa. xlv. 24, 25, "Surely, shall one say, In the Lord have I righteousness and strength.—In the Lord shall all the seed of Israel be justified, and shall glory."

(3.) Eye the conscience-purging blood, Heb. xii. 22, 24. If thou hast come up into Christ's chariot of the covenant, the covering of it is a covert of purple, that is ever over thy head. When conscience is wounded with guilt, it is like a thorn got into the foot of the traveller, who can walk no more till it be drawn out, Heb. ix. 14.

4. Eye him as the fountain of strength, Isa. xlv. 24, forecited. This is the way that David resolved to walk with God, Psalm lxxi. 16, "I will go in the strength of the Lord God." The way we have to go is difficult, we have little strength, and there is much opposition; we need to keep our eye on him in whom the believer's strength lies, Psalm lxxxiv. 5. None walk with God but those that draw strength from him, for the whole of their walk. And that lies in two things.

(1.) Believing the promise of strength and furniture, for whatever piece of the way we are called to go through, Psalm cxvi. 9, 10, "I will walk before the Lord in the land of the living. I believed, therefore have I spoken." The spiritual traveller has many a difficult step in his way to Immanuel's land, but in the covenant there is strength promised to carry him through them all. He must keep his eye on the promise, and firmly believe it, for that is the way to suck the breasts of these consolations.

(2.) Using the means on the credit of the promise. God's institutions have promises annexed to them, and they become effectual, being thus believingly used; Heb. iv. 2, compare John xvii. 17. To pretend to believe without the use of means, is presumption; to use the means without believing the promise, is lifeless formality. Is there a lust to mortify, or a temptation to resist? let us use the means, and believe the promise of sanctification with close application to ourselves.

5. Eye him as our Master, Lord, head, and husband; Psalm xlv. 11, "He is thy Lord, and worship thou him." See how the spouse comes out of the wilderness walking with God, even leaning on him as her Head and Husband; Cant. viii. 5. We must walk with him, as obedient servants with a master, dutiful subjects with a king, &c. Whomsoever others serve, let it be our resolution to serve the Lord; Josh. xxiv. 15. And this imports, that we must be ready,

(1.) To receive his orders, and the least indications of his mind to comply with them, signified to us by his word or providence. How closely did the psalmist thus walk with God? Psalm cxxiii. 2, "Behold, as the eyes of servants look unto the hands of their masters, and as the eyes of a maiden unto the hand of her mistress; so our eyes wait upon the Lord our God, until that he have mercy upon us." And this is the duty of all pretending to be espoused to Christ. So that it must needs be great untenderness, that "God speaks once, yea, twice, yet men regard it not."

(2.) To do his bidding; "Lord, what wilt thou have me to do?" said Paul; Acts ix. 6. Our Lord lets us see, that it is not talking of, but thus walking with God, that is religion indeed; Luke vi. 46, "Why call ye me Lord, Lord, and do not the things which I say?" And it is not the hearers, but the doers of the word that shall be justified. There is no walking with God, if we walk not in the road of obedience to his commands. If we take our own way, we walk not with him, but Satan.

(3.) To be careful to please him in all things; 1 Cor. vii. 34, to give content to the heart of Christ in whatever we do; Col. i. 10, not only to do the thing he commands, but to do it to his mind, so as he may take pleasure in us, and delight to do us good. For thus the duty of Christ's spouse in walking with God is summed up; Psalm xlv. 10, "Hearken, O daughter, and consider, and incline thine ear; forget also thine own people, and thy father's house."

6. *Lastly*. Eye him as our chief end. As he that walks with God

sets off in his way in him and by him, so he walks to him as the great end of his walk; Psalm xvi. 8, "I have set the Lord always before me." Rom. xi. *ult.*, "For of him, and through him, and to him are all things; to whom be glory for ever. Amen." This implies two things,

(1.) Aiming at his glory in all things; 1 Cor. x. 31. We must make that the great scope of all our actions, and of our whole life. He that walks with God displaces self, which is the dead sea into which all our actions naturally run, and sets up the honour of God instead thereof; reckoning his life no more useful in the world than it tends to the honour of God. For we are as trees in a vineyard, of no use, but as they bring forth fruit to their master's use; Luke xiii. 7.

(2.) Seeking to enjoy him as our chief happiness; Psalm lxxiii. 25. Man can never be self-sufficient, (no not angels); that is the peculiar prerogative of God, whose perfections are infinite. So he must needs seek his happiness without himself. While he is without God in a natural state, he seeks it in the creatures; when he comes to God, he takes God for it. And walking with God, he habitually seeks it in the enjoyment of him, and feeds at that table he sits down to in conversion. And so if ye would walk with God,

(1.) Ye must seek to enjoy him in all things, in the measure he is to be enjoyed here; Psalm xxvii. 4; seek to enjoy him in ordinances; Psalm lxiii. 1, 2, public, private, and secret. Ye must not stay in the shell, nor in the outer court; but seek to believe, taste, and feel; Psalm xxxiv. 8. Ye must seek him in providences; Psalm xciv. 4, merciful and favourable, smiling and frowning. He will be the sap and foyson of mercies to the walker with God; Gen. xxxiii. 10, and they will see his name in cross dispensations; Micah vi. 9.

(2.) Ye must seek to enjoy him in heaven hereafter. If ye walk through the world with God, ye will walk as pilgrims bound for another and better country, keeping that in your view as your only rest; Heb. xi. 13, 16. He that walks with God, walks as one living that he may die well, making it the business of this life that he may learn to die, and to get beyond it to a better life.

Secondly. We must walk with God in the way of the heart's going along with him in all things, as the shadow goes with the body. Hence it is called "walking after the Lord;" Hos. xi. 10, "following the Lord;" Numb. xiv. 24. Walking with God is no bodily motion, but a spiritual motion, a moving of the heart and affections; and so it must import necessarily the heart's going along with him. I will take it up in these three things. If ye would walk with God, your hearts must go along with him,

1. In the way of believing in all things. Thus Enoch walked with God; Heb. xi. 5. God is a Spirit, and our souls are spirits. The way of communion betwixt God and us is in the way of believing, for we cannot know him to our salvation, but as he has revealed himself to us in his word. So God manifesting himself by his word, we cannot walk with him, but as our hearts go along with these manifestations of himself, in the way of believing; hence is that account the apostle gives us of his walk; Gal. ii. 20, " The life which I now live in the flesh, I live by the faith of the Son of God, who loved me, and gave himself for me." So walking with God imports,

(1.) Believing his commands. Faith discerns the stamp of divine authority on the commands, and so gives them a suitable weight on one's own spirit. It esteems and judges them all right and reasonable; Psalm cxix. 128. So they are believed to be not only from God, but suited to the divine perfections, and to man's real welfare. Which cannot miss to influence the person to obedience.

(2.) Believing his promises, the promises of the gospel; Heb. xi. 13. He that walks with God, does not only believe the great leading promises of the covenant, of God himself's being their God, and of eternal salvation, but the lesser promises depending on these. And while others take other things for their heritage, they take the promises for theirs; Psalm cxix. 111. So the great thing that sways them in their course of life, is the prospect of unseen things; (2 Cor. iv. 18,) to be had in another world, and likewise the prospect of what is promised even in this life.

So the promises are apt to influence obedience; and when they do, that is walking with God; when one ventures on, and follows the way of duty on the credit of the promise; *e.g.* giving out of their substance at God's call, upon the faith of the promise; Prov. iii. 9, 10, &c.

(3.) Believing his threatenings; Heb. xi. 7. We find holy men have thus walked with God, being influenced to a tender holy walk by the faith of God's threatenings in his word; Job xxxii. ult. David was not of a servile legal spirit, when he says, Psalm cxix. 120, " My flesh trembleth for fear of thee, and I am afraid of thy judgments." Hence they that walk with God, will not venture on an ill thing, more than they would take fire into their bosom, because the terror of God makes them afraid of sin.

2. In the way of compliance with his holy will. If we do not thus in all things, we walk contrary to him. When man fell off from God, his own will became his law, and was set in opposition to

the will of God. When he returns to God, his will is inclined by grace to God's will; and walking with God it goes along therewith, complying with it in all things. So walking with God imports,

(1.) Complying with the will of his command in all things; Acts ix. 6. The heart of the believer is reconciled to, and approves of the law as holy, just, and good; and while he walks with God, he labours sincerely to suit his walk thereunto in all things, being grieved at any reluctancy that is in the heart against any piece of obedience, crying with David, Psalm cxix. 5, "O that my ways were directed to keep thy statutes!"

(2.) Complying with the will of his providence, the heart being reconciled to that lot which God is pleased to carve out; Psalm xlvii. 4. O what walking contrary to God is there in this respect, while the proud unhumbled heart will not, cannot accommodate itself to divine dispensations! but murmurs, frets, and repines, and rebels against the Lord, as the sovereign Governor of the world.

3. In the way of habitual moving of the heart towards him. Grace has an attractive virtue in the heart drawing it towards God. And when it is in exercise, it will make the heart to be moving towards him, whereas otherwise it settles on other things besides him. So in walking with God there is,

(1.) Frequent thinking and meditating on him, Mal. iii. 16. That is a black character of the wicked; Psalm x. 4, "God is not in all his thoughts." And the saint is in a backgoing condition that begins to forget him; Jer. ii. 32. Yea, fleeting thoughts are not sufficient; if we walk with God, he will be the subject of our meditation, both occasional and stated; Psalm lxiii. 6. If we walk with a man, he is ever in our view, and so we cannot miss to think on him.

(2.) Habitual moving of the heart towards him, in love, desire, trust, &c. He is the chief good and the best of beings, which should ever command our love, Deut. vi. 5. That is the holy fire that is kept glowing and flaming in the heart of one that walks with God, loving him for himself, and for his goodness to us. Desires after him are the breathings of a soul touched with the love of God, tending to perfect enjoyment. And the continual wants and weakness that such a one finds himself compassed with, turn him very naturally to trust and dependence on him.

(3.) Frequent use of ejaculatory prayer, 1 Thes. v. 17. This is that kind of prayer to which we have access at all times, the darting up of a desire to the Lord, whatever be the lawful business we are about, or whatever be our case. And hardly can people be thought to walk with God, that are not frequently sending these swift, though silent, messengers to heaven. We find Jacob, in the midst of his testament, using such a devout ejaculation; Gen. xlix. 18, "I have waited for thy salvation, O Lord." See Moses's practice, Exod. xiv. 15, and Nehemiah's, before he answered a king, Neh. ii. 4.

Thirdly, We must walk with God in ordinances, Luke i. 6, submitting to, and seeking communion with God in all ordinances as we have access. The ordinances are the banqueting-house of Christ wherein he feasts his people, Cant. ii. 4, the galleries wherein the king is held by those that walk with him there, Cant. vii. 5. Particularly the communion with God is to be sought and kept up,

1. In secret prayer, Matth. vi. 6. We must walk with God in a due and ordinary observance of that kind of prayer. It is a duty wherein the people of God have had as much communion with God as in any other; witness Jacob's experience, Gen. xxxii. 24, and Daniel's, chap. ix. 22. The Lord promises his people a particular familiarity with him in that duty; Cant. vii. 11, "Come, my beloved, let us go forth into the field; let us lodge in the villages." And however some may be blythe to get it shifted, yet the truly-exercised would find it hard, nay, they could not at all live without it. And how people can walk with God, taking it only now and then, and not making conscience of ordinary observing of it, I see not. And indeed people will readily know by their disposition in secret prayer, whether they be in a thriving case or not.

2. In family prayer, Acts x. 2, 3. Never one that gives Christ heart-room, but they will be willing to give him house-room too. And there are none that walk with God themselves, but they would fain all their family walked with God too, Josh xxiv. 15. And there are none who have gone about it seriously, but must say, that family worship is an ordinance in which God is to be found. Prayerless families are in a dangerous condition; they are as if the owners should uncover the roofs of them, that wrath may be showered down on them; Jer. x. *ult.*, "Pour out thy fury upon the heathen that know thee not, and upon the families that call not on thy name." And I think if people were walking with God in family-duties, they would not lay by the morning-exercise, as many of you do. And what is it that hinders it? What but the weary world? Ye cannot get time for it, because of your business. But are ye not afraid of God's curse on that business that shuts out his worship? And if it should thrive, ye take the way to get leanness to your souls. It looks not like walking with God to stand off from family worship, till they have no other thing ado, and it is a graceless-like thing to offer only that time to God that costs you nothing.

3. In reading of the word, John v. 39. We find the truly-godly have been great lovers of the Bible. O how does David commend it, especially in the 119th psalm, though it was but a small part of it that was written in his time. One that would walk with God, should even walk through the Bible, reading it, and acquainting themselves with the mind of God in it. And ye will see, that whenever persons come to be in earnest exercised about their case, they will very naturally go to their Bibles in quite another manner than they used to do.

4. In extraordinary prayer, setting time apart for it, either in secret, or in families; of which I have spoken before.*

5. In hearing the word. Whenever the Lord puts an occasion of hearing the word in your hand, he says in effect, Come walk with me in the galleries; and " with joy shall ye draw water out of the wells of salvation," Isa. xii. 3. And every believing soul will reply with David, Psalm lxv. 4, " Blessed is the man whom thou choosest, and causest to approach unto thee, that he may dwell in thy courts: we shall be satisfied with the goodness of thy house, even of thy holy temple." The Sabbath-day is a day of blessing, the preaching of the gospel is the great means for the salvation of sinners, 1 Cor. i. 21. Is it not then a slighting of communion with God, for people to idle away so many Sabbaths at home, in making so little conscience of attending on public ordinances? Read through the whole Bible, and ye will not find a gracious person but was much addicted to the place where his honour dwells, to public ordinances. And I assure you, the godly in some places would wonder if they could have any good in them at all, that can contentedly sit at home, when they are neither sick nor sore, nor have any providential necessity put upon them. It is very observable, Numb. ix. 10—13, " that if any man of Israel, or of their posterity should be unclean by reason of a dead body, or be in a journey afar off, yet he should keep the passover unto the Lord:—but the man that was clean, and was not in a journey, and forebore to keep the passover; even the same soul should be cut off from his people, because he brought not the offering of the Lord in his appointed season." Whence observe, that as those who against their wills are forced to be absent from God's ordinances, may expect the favours of his grace under their affliction; so those who of choice absent themselves, may expect the tokens of his wrath for their sin.

6. *Lastly.* In the sacrament of the Lord's supper. That is an ordinance especially appointed for communion with God; 1 Cor. x. 16.

---

* See Memorial concerning personal and family fasting, annexed to the author's View of the Covenant of Grace.

And it has been so in the experience of many souls. Wherefore it must be strange how those can walk with God, that never set their foot on that holy ground, though they have one opportunity after another.

And if ye would walk with God in these duties, (1.) Ye must make conscience of preparation, even prepare for secret prayer, &c. (2.) Seek and press forward for communion with God in these ordinances, and take not up with the external work. (3.) Do not take them by starts, but keep an ordinary, as ye have occasion, otherwise ye cannot be said to walk with God in them.

FOURTHLY. We must walk with God in providences. These are his ways wherein he walks towards us, and we must walk with him in them; Hos. xiv. ult., "Who is wise, and he shall understand these things? prudent, and he shall know them? for the ways of the Lord are right, and the just shall walk in them." Sometimes he goes with us in the way of smiling, sometimes of cross providences; but whether he take the high road of lifting up, or the low one of downcasting, we are to follow, and walk with him. This lies in these seven things,

1. We must notice his hand in all that we meet with from any hand whatsoever. God guides the world by wisdom, and without him second causes cannot move; Ezek. i. 20. Whether thou meet with a mercy or a cross, say in thine heart, This is the finger of God; Gen. xxxiii. 10. The not noticing of this is a spice of atheism, that God is highly displeased with; Psalm xxviii. 5, "Because they regard not the works of the Lord, nor the operation of his hands, he shall destroy them, and not build them up." See how the Pagan Chaldeans do with smiling providences; Hab. i. 16, "They sacrifice unto their net, and burn incense unto their drag; because by them their portion is fat, and their meat plenteous." And see what the Philistines say of their afflictions, "It is a chance." But he that walketh with God, takes all out of the Lord's hand.

2. We must accommodate ourselves to the aspect of providence, whether it be shining or louring; Eccl. vii. 14. For without this we shew a contempt of providence, which the Lord takes heinously, as you may see by looking to Isa. xxii. 12—14. We must rejoice in his mercies, and walk soberly and concernedly under the strokes of his hand.

3. We must labour to find out the design of providence. Providence has a voice, and it is a voice of speech which may be understood; Ezek. i. 24. The works of providence are a book which the walker with God labours to read the mind of God in. Merciful dispensations are preachers of repentance, and happy are they that

hear their voice; Rom. ii. 4. Cross dispensations have a language to the same purpose; Micah vi. 9, "The Lord's voice crieth unto the city, and the man of wisdom shall see thy name; hear ye the rod, and who hath appointed it."

To help you to know the particular design of providence in cross dispensations that ye meet with.

(1.) Pray in faith for it, believing that God will discover it to you in the use of means, in his own time; Job x. 2, "Shew me wherefore thou contendest with me." Compare Matth. xxi. 22, "All things whatsoever ye shall ask in prayer, believing, ye shall receive." But take good heed that your souls be truly and honestly laid open to divine instruction, that you be disposed to know it at any rate, though it should touch you in a most sensible part; Psalm xxv. 9, "The meek will he guide in judgment; and the meek will he teach his way."

(2.) Search for it, as the Israelites did for the accursed thing; Psalm lxxvii. 6. Think upon it, in order to find it out. Take a view of your way, what it was before and at the time when ye met with the cross; even as when men have lost any thing, they go back till they come to the place where they are sure they had it.

(3.) Take help of the word in this matter. Consider scripture-threatenings, or examples, that may be apposite to your case. All that you or I meet with is but a fulfilling of the scripture; Hos. vii. 12. And as providence gives light to the word, so the word gives light to providence. And thus Moses opened up the meaning of a dark providence to Aaron from the word; Lev. x. 3, "This is it that the Lord spake, saying, I will be sanctified in them that come nigh me, and before all the people I will be glorified. And Aaron held his peace."

(4.) Listen to the whispers of conscience under the rod. The sin that under the rod conscience casts most in thy teeth, is very likely to be the sin that God is aiming at, as in the case of Joseph's brethren; Gen. xlii. 21, who "said one to another, We are verily guilty concerning our brother, in that we saw the anguish of his soul, when he besought us; and we would not hear; therefore is this distress come upon us." Even as the man that has a sore finger, whatever touches his hand, the finger smarts; an evidence that there his sore lies.

(5.) Consider what sin it is that thou hast had most reproofs for from the word, most checks for by some lesser steps of providence, most challenges for from conscience, and yet thou hast not reformed. That is likely to be it. For God's rods follow his rebukes, as Absalom did with Joab: Jer. xxii. 21, 22, "I spake unto thee in thy prosperity, but thou saidst, I will not hear; this hath been thy manner from thy youth, that thou obeyest not my voice. The wind shall eat up all thy pastures, and thy lovers shall go into captivity, surely then shalt thou be ashamed and confounded for all thy wickedness."

6. *Lastly.* Consider the nature of the stroke or cross, for very readily there is a discernable affinity betwixt sin and the stroke. Sometimes God punishes men in the same kind with their sin, as in the case of Adonibezek; Judg. i. 7. Sometimes in the occasion of their sins, as Eli's indulgence to his children was punished by the death of them. Sometimes their punishment is in what is most contrary to their sin, as David's sin in numbering of the people. Sometimes God measures to us in temporals, as we do to him in spirituals; Hos. iv. 12, 13; 1 Cor. xi. 30, and several other ways.

One that walks with God will have so much ado with these things, that they should very carefully observe them, for daily practice of taking up God's mind in what they meet with.

4. We must endeavour to comply with the designs of providence; Job xxxvi. 10, 11. Providences in favourable dispensations are God's cords of love and bands of a man, whereby he draws sinners to himself. In afflicting dispensations they are God's furnace for melting of souls, that they may take on suitable impressions. And O but it is sad when the effect of all is that; Hos. xi. 2, "As they called them, so they went from them." Jer. vi. 29, 30, "The bellows are burnt, the lead is consumed of the fire, the founder melteth in vain; for the wicked are not plucked away. Reprobate silver shall men call them, because the Lord hath rejected them." That is a grievous complaint; Jer. v. 3, "Thou hast stricken them, but they have not grieved; thou hast consumed them, but they have refused to receive correction; they have made their faces harder than a rock, they have refused to return." But he that walketh with God makes it his business to comply with the dispensations of providence in the design of them, to serve the Lord more cheerfully that God is kind to him, and to bring forth the peaceable fruits of righteousness under afflictions.

5. We must notice the harmony of providences with the word; Psalm xlviii. 8, "As we have heard, so have we seen in the city of the Lord of hosts." This is the way to get communion with God in providences. And a sweet feast they often afford to those that are thus exercised to discern them; hence, says David; Psalm xcii. 4, "Thou, Lord, hast made me glad through thy work. I will triumph in the works of thy hands?" and said Jacob to his brother Esau; Gen. xxxiii. 10, "Therefore have I seen thy face, as though I had seen the face of God, and thou wast pleased with me." The

word is the scheme and draught of the government of the world; and the lines of providence are all drawn accordingly. So that whatsoever thou meetest with, it is an accomplishment of scripture-promises, threatenings and doctrines. And a child of God in applying them thus to the rule, may have sweet communion with God.

6. We must follow the conduct of providence in subserviency to the word, keeping our eye on the promise; Psalm xxxii. 8, " I will instruct thee, and teach thee in the way which thou shalt go; I will guide thee with mine eye." To separate providence from the word, and then make it a rule, is dangerous; Jonah i. 3. But to follow the conduct of it with an eye to the word, is a notable part of the Christian's walking with God. Providence is the hand of the Lord whereby he opens the way in the wilderness to his people, that they may follow him. And go where they will, as long as they can thus keep their eye on their guide, they may judge themselves in the safest way.

7. *Lastly.* We must live in the exercise of the graces suitable to the dispensations of providence wherewith we are trysted; Eccl. vii. 14. Some dispensations are sweet and comfortable; let us by them be stirred up to love the Lord the more; Psalm cxvi. 1. Let any comfort that we find in the creature be used to enlarge our hearts in thankfulness to, desire of, and cheerfulness in serving the Lord. Some are heavy, and require patience; some dark and doubtful, and require faith. Some take away our created supports, and dry up our cisterns, and put out our candle; and such require trust in the Lord, and to rejoice in him; Hab. iii. 17, 18. Thus he that walks with God, follows him whithersoever he goes.

FIFTHLY, We must walk with God in the stations and relations wherein he hath placed us. These are the sphere that God hath given us to move in, in the world. And whoso walks not with God in them, will never please him. There are two pieces of work which a Christian has to do.

1. One for himself, and that is his salvation-work; Phil. ii. 12. That is, to secure his eternal welfare in the enjoyment of God, so to make sure his gracious state, to maintain a gracious frame and disposition, by getting incident controversies betwixt God and his soul done away, grace actuated, strengthened, and nourished, till he come to the stature of a perfect man in Christ. This lies in his personal walk.

2. One for God, and that is his generation-work; Acts xiii. 36. This lies in his relative walk. Whence we may conclude, that so far as a man or woman is defective in their relative duties, so far they are useless for God, and take up room in the world for no pur-

pose. And so far as they do ill instead of good in their relations, they walk contrary to God. We see how the Lord in the works of nature has joined together the creatures, the sun to shine by day, and the moon by night, the beasts to serve man, and the earth with the products thereof to serve both. The beauty of the world lies in every one's keeping their place, and being serviceable in the place wherein God has set them. And so relations are the joints of society; and they that would walk with God, must walk with him in them.

(1.) We must labour faithfully to discharge the duties of our stations and relations, as under the eye of God, who is our common Overseer, Witness, and Judge; Psalm ci. 2. God has shaped out our work to us, whether in the church, commonwealth, or family, wherein some are as eyes, some as hands, and some as feet. Though the work of others may be higher and more honourable than ours, our greatest honour will be to approve ourselves to God in our own part. God observes how every one does his duty, the husband, the wife, the master, the servant. And they that walk with God, will behave themselves in these things as under the eye of God, as well as when they are at prayers; &c. Col. iii. 22.

(2.) We must do the duties of our relations under a sense of the command of God. It is not enough that the husband love his wife, or the wife submit herself to her husband, &c., if conscience of duty towards God do not sway them thereto; Eph. v. 21. We must make God our great party in all these things, otherwise we do not walk with God in them. There is no relation one stands in, but God has set them their duty; and so the performance of these duties is as much the trial of our obedience, as the most religious actions we are capable of.

(3.) We must do the duties of our relations with an eye to the real good of our relatives. "Thou shalt love thy neighbour as thyself," is the sum of the second table. No man is born for himself, but to be serviceable to God and his fellow-creatures; Rom. xv. 2. And the more useful we are to others, the more we serve God, and the more we are like him; for he does good unto all, even unto the unholy and unthankful.

(4.) *Lastly.* We must do the duties of our relations with an eye to the honour of God; 1 Cor. x. 31. O the dishonour that is done to God by the little conscience that is made of relative duties, by crying relative sins. Should the fabric of the world run into confusion, sun, moon, stars, day and night, go out of their courses, where were the honour of God arising from the beauty of an orderly management of the world? But ah! how often are the foundations in churches, states, and families out of course, and there nothing but disorder and confusion, contention and opposition, every one going out of their course; and so the honour of God, and their own good and comfort lying buried in the ruinous heap? This is walking contrary to God.

This walking with God is particularly noticed concerning Enoch; Gen. v. 22, "And Enoch walked with God after he begat Methuselah three hundred years, and begat sons and daughters." He walked with God in his family, as a father and a husband, in the married state. So if thou be a walker with God, it will appear in the relations wherein thou standest; for grace makes a good husband, a good wife, a good master, a good servant, &c. And the duties of relations will readily try both the reality and strength of grace.

SIXTHLY, We must walk with God in all our actions, whether natural, civil, or religious; 1 Cor. x. 31, "Whether therefore ye eat or drink, or whatsoever ye do, do all to the glory of God." Religion is to our conversation like salt to meat, necessary to season our whole life, whatever it is that we are about.

First, We must walk with God in our natural actions, such as eating, drinking, sleeping, &c. These are common to us with the beasts; but we must not be like the beasts in the use of them, but walk with God therein. Now, if we would walk with God in these things,

1. We must do them under a sense of the command of God. Eating and drinking, &c., are duties of the sixth command; and therefore we ought to do them because God has said, "Thou shalt not kill." Wherever there is a divine ordinance respecting any natural action, we ought therein to have respect to that ordinance; 1 Tim. iv. 4, 5, "For every creature of God is good, and nothing to be refused, if it be received with thanksgiving; for it is sanctified by the word of God and prayer." Our bodies are the Lord's, and he binds us by all lawful means to preserve them; and then do men walk with God in these things, while they patch up the mud-wall house under the sense of the command of the owner.

2. We must depend on the Lord for benefit by them; 1 Tim. iv. 5. Without the blessing on the means, the end cannot be obtained. Without God our meat cannot nourish us, nor our clothes warm us; so that the emptiness of the creature points us to God at every turn, agreeable to what our Lord says; Matth. iv. 4, "Man shall not live by bread alone, but by every word that proceedeth out of the mouth of God." It is no less than spiritual idolatry to overlook the Lord, and look for the benefit from the creature itself; Jer. xvii. 5; Hos. iv. 10. If he would say the word, we might eat and not be filled, sleep and not be refreshed. So that even in these we are called to

walk by faith with God, looking for the benefit of God's ordinance and appointment about these things.

3. We must use them for God and his service; as the traveller takes his staff in his hand, not to be a burden or a carriage to him, but to help him on his journey. While the soul is in the body, it has a mighty dependence thereon; and so it is as the horse that must be cared for, to the end we may accomplish the journey; 2 Kings iii. 15. So walking with God in these things, would make us use them so, as may most fit us for the work of our Christian calling, having that as our great scope before our eye.

4. We must keep a holy Christian moderation in these things; Phil. iv. 5. We must be like Gideon's lappers, even when waters of a full cup are set before us. People may easily fall into a sinful eagerness in these things; Gen. xxv. 30, and sink their hearts into these things, wherein they should only lightly go along with wariness; Luke xxi. 31, regulating ourselves in the use of them, by what is best to fit us for our salvation and generation-work, which is the true rule of moderation. For the heart must not sit down on them as its end and rest; but pass through them as a means and way; 1 Cor. vii. 29—31.

5. We must ascend by the creature unto the Creator, from creature-sweetness to that infinite fulness that is in God; Zech. ix. *ult.*, "How great is his goodness, and how great is his beauty! corn shall make the young men cheerful, and new wine the maids." Seeing all perfection in the creature is originally from God, it must be in him, and that infinitely. If there be any thing desirable in the streams, it must be more so in the fountain. If the light of the sun be so pleasant to the eyes, he who is light itself must be infinitely more so. Whatever pleasure or delight we find in meat, drink, &c. it points us to God, from whom that sweetness is derived, as drops from the ocean.

6. We must look on them as covenant mercies, and the fulfilment of promises; Deut. xxvi. 3, &c. God has secured our necessary comforts by promise; Isa. xxxiii. 16. "Bread shall be given him, his waters shall be sure." Psalm cxxvii. 2, and lxxxiv. 11. So when we receive them, we should look on them as such; and then however coarse the meat be, being served up in the dish, not of common providence, but of the covenant, it will have an uncommon sweetness, and we will have communion with God in that which others find no more in than beasts do.

7. *Lastly.* We must be thankful for all our mercies, unto God as the giver; 1 Thess. v. 18. We must pay to him verbal acknowledgements; Hos. xiv. 2; Deut. viii. 10, and real acknowledgements,

serving him in the strength of our mercies, and that cheerfully, as he deals graciously with us in these things. What we have from him must be used for him; Rom. xi. *ult.*; and the more liberally he deals with us, the more cheerfully ought we to serve him; Deut. xxviii. 47, 48.

Secondly. We must walk with God in our civil actions, such as are competent to men in society, as trading, buying, selling, working, and in a word, managing our worldly business: that as we may not act like beasts in the former, so we may not act as men that know not God in the latter. Now, if we would walk with God in managing of our temporal affairs,

1. We must act in these matters as under a sense of a command or appointment of God in them. God has given each his calling, station, and work; and we are to act therein suitably in obedience to him; 1 Cor. vii. 24, doing our proper business as to the Lord, who is our great Master; Eph. vi. 7. Thus a man should go about his worldly business, whether for his own or another's advantage because God has said, "Thou shalt not steal;" looking on it as a piece of his duty to God.

2. We must depend on him by faith, for direction in our business; Prov. iii. 6. We must pray for it, and trust God for it. Temporal affairs are not excepted; Phil. iv. 6, "In every thing by prayer and supplication with thanksgiving, let your requests be made known unto God." Whence is a dexterity and skill to manage a temporal business, to do a piece of work to purpose without or within doors? Is it not from the Lord? Jam. i. 17, "Every good gift, and every perfect gift is from above." Isa. xxviii. 26, "For his God doth instruct him to discretion, and doth teach him." Common influences of the Spirit are as necessary to the exercise of a gift, as saving influences are to the exercise of grace. Remember the error the princes of Israel fell into; Josh. ix. 14, "The men took of their victuals, and asked not counsel at the mouth of the Lord;" and Lot's unhappy choice, wherein he did not own God; Gen. xiii. 11, 12.

3. We must depend on the Lord by faith, for the success of our lawful endeavours; Psalm cxxvii. 1. Whatever men undertake with an eye to God in it, they may depend on him for the success of it; Psalm i. 3. An unsanctified confidence of success God often blasts, that he may let all men see in every thing, that "by strength no man shall prevail;" 1 Sam. ii. 9, and that "the race is not to the swift, nor the battle to the strong;" Eccl. ix. 11. And while people torment themselves with anxiety as to events, he brings their fears ofttimes on them, and lets them see, that by taking thought no man can add a cubit to his stature.

4. We must cut and carve in them as may be most for the honour of God and our soul's welfare. This is the great mark that we would always keep in view, and according to which we must steer our course. Our eternal interest is our greatest, and all other interests must vail to it. The honour of God is the sheaf to which all others must bow; and the balance is to be cast on that side always on which these are; Matth. xvi. 26, "For what is a man profited, if he shall gain the whole world, and lose his own soul? or what shall a man give in exchange for his soul?" Where is the gain where the foot is lost to save the shoe? The world, with whom gain is godliness, and a penny more or less determines them in their affairs, would have thought Moses a foolish man for missing a good bargain; Heb. xi. 24. But he acted even as wisely, as a man who cares not for gaining that pound, in gaining which he must lose a talent. Therefore consider in your worldly affairs, what will be best for your souls.

5. We must deal with men as under the eye of God, a holy jealous God, whether we be masters, servants, neighbours, &c. Eph. v. 15. Be strict and precise observers of common justice, according to the golden rule, "Whatsoever ye would that men should do unto you, do ye even so unto them." Whatever occasions you have to do an unjust thing, let the eye of God be a sufficient restraint; Job xxxi. 21—23. Let men pretend to what strictness they will otherwise, while they are not strict in their morals this way, they do more ill to religion, than perhaps they will ever be capable to do good.

6. We must observe Christian moderation in these things; 1 Cor. vii. 29, 30. Do not give yourselves wholly to them, to relish nothing but what savours of them, as those of Solomon did; Luke xvii. 28. Let them not steal away your heart, and justle out religion, like those mentioned, Luke xiv. 16, &c., but remember still you have greater business in hand than that; and therefore dip no farther into them, than you may do with safety to your soul's case.

7. *Lastly.* We must be suitably affected with the providence of God in these things; ascribing the success of our affairs to the Lord, and giving him thanks for blessing the work of our hands; acknowledging disappointments and crosses in them to come from the same hand; taking them kindly as trials wherewith the Lord sees meet to exercise us, and labouring to know and comply with the design of them.

Thirdly, We must walk with God in our religious actions, and so distinguish ourselves from hypocrites, who do the things, pray, hear, &c., but do not walk with God in them. Now, if we would walk with God in religious duties,

1. We must do our duty out of respect to the command of God; Psalm cxix. 4. We must say in this case, as Simon did in another; Luke v. 5, "At thy word I will let down the net." When people are led to duties from a custom, or some such low principles or motives, they do not walk with God in them. He that walks with God in them, discerns the stamp of divine authority on every duty, and that awes his heart into a compliance therewith.

2. We must seek the honour of God in all we do; John viii. 50. And indeed if we be let into a view of his glory in duties, the advancing of it will be our great aim. If thou be in duty with others, let God himself be your scope, and take heed of parting the glory betwixt him and thyself. If thou be alone, seek to give him the glory of all his perfections, by acknowledging of, and carrying as under the impression of, the same.

3. We must go about our duty in his own strength; Zech. x. *ult.*; Psalm lxxi. 16, renouncing all confidence in ourselves; 2 Cor. iii. 5. No gifts are to be trusted to in this, for they may soon be blasted, and no bare gift can make one act graciously. Nay, habitual grace is not to be trusted to for that end; for the fire not blown cannot give us light. Actual grace needs still to be preserved and fed, else it will fail. Therefore we must lean on the Lord himself for it; Isa. xlv. 24. And we must stretch out the withered hand in duty, in hopes of influences from him, and set to sea in confidence of the blowings of the Spirit.

4. We must be spiritual in our duties; John iv. 24; Phil. iii. 3. One that walks with God will not take up with bodily exercise, or lip-labour; but endeavour after inward worship, which is the work of the heart. This lies in loving, fearing, trusting, desiring, humbling of the heart before him; believing his word, &c. And so he will reckon no more to be done in worship of God, than what is done with the heart.

5. We must seek to enjoy God in duties, and not be satisfied without it; Psalm xxvii. 4. When thou comest to the galleries, let thine aim be to see the King in his glory. And let not the empty chair of state satisfy thy soul; for nothing is sufficient for the soul, but the enjoyment of God himself; Psalm lxxiii. 25. And if this be thine aim, thou wilt pursue it, and thurst forward till thou come even to his seat.

6. We must carry in duties as under the eye of God, in a special manner; Psalm lxxxix. 7, "God is greatly to be feared in the assembly of the saints; and to be had in reverence of all them that are about him." That looseness of heart, whereby it wanders here and there at duty, proceeds from the want of a due fear of God

upon the soul; and is most contrary to walking with God; Jer. xii. 2, "Thou art near in their mouth, and far from their reins." The fixing of the heart under the impressions of his awful presence, that so the soul may carry suitably before him, is to sanctify the Lord in our heart; Lev. x. 3.

7. We must be frequent in duties; 1 Thess. v. 17. They that walk with God are frequent in solemn duties; but in the interval of these they will be taken up with others of a less solemn nature, such as thinking, meditation on God, ejaculations, &c. And thus they will be readily kept in tune for the return of the more solemn duties. And indeed people then cease to walk with God, when they begin to be more remiss and infrequent in solemn duties, and to be less careful of the frame of their hearts in the interval.

8. We must let new occurrences send us to our duty. This has been the practice of walkers with God, that whatever they have met with remarkable, it sent them to God? and "therefore," says the prophet, "I will look unto the Lord; I will wait for the God of my salvation; my God will hear me;" Micah vii. 7. And where can a gracious heart have such a vent, as before the Lord, whatever it be full of, whether joy or grief?

9. *Lastly.* We must observe the fruit of our duties; Psalm v. 3, carefully notice what speed we come in our applications to the throne; and what effect God's speaking upon his throne has upon us. This is communion with God, to be sending word to, and receiving word from heaven; to be importing something thither in duties and the exercise of grace, and to be exporting something thence for the spiritual enriching of the soul.

THIRDLY, I shall consider walking with God in the properties thereof. Walking with God is religion; and it is,

1. Practical religion, religion in deed, not in word only; and there is no other sort of religion that will bring us to heaven; hence says our Lord; John xiii. 17, "If ye know these things, happy are ye if ye do them." Talk as we will, if we do not walk with God, we are naught. Jacob dissembling with his father was the lively emblem of a hypocrite, the voice Jacob's, the hands Esau's. There is a great difference betwixt saying and doing in religion. The former is easy, the latter is difficult.

(1.) One may talk well of God and the things of God, and yet have nothing of the truth of religion. He may have a clear head in matters of religion, that has a dark heart; he may have a ready tongue to speak of them, whose feet are shackled with divers lusts, that he cannot walk in the way he speaks of; 1 Cor. xiii. 2. How many are ready in the history of the Bible, that are strangers to the mystery of practical godliness? It is said of Cleopatra, queen of Egypt, that people were chained to her rather by the ear than by the eyes. So many, if ye hear them speak, they are something; but if ye look to their life, they are naught.

(2.) One may talk well for God, and yet have nothing of the truth of religion. But though they talk for him, they walk contrary to him. A man may preach for God, and teach others the way, that yet he never sets his foot on himself; Matth. xxiii. 4. Being like a boatman that ferries others over the water, but still with his own back towards the shore. Both ministers and professors may contend zealously for the faith of doctrine, while they are utter strangers to the life of faith; like a physician prescribing remedies to others, while himself is dying of his disease, without applying of proper remedies.

(3.) One may talk well to God, that yet never walks with him. Many speak fair to the Lord, whose walk is ever foul, never cleansed; as in Israel's case; Deut. v. 27, 29. Fair professions, resolutions, promises, are often seen going up as dust. Look to their words, they are like Naphthali giving goodly words, but still as Rachel, though beautiful yet barren; Matth. vii. 21, " Not every one that saith unto me, Lord, Lord, shall enter into the kingdom of heaven."

But religion being a practical thing, let no man think he has begun to be religious, till he come to practice; Jam. ii. 16, 17.—" faith, if it hath not works, is dead being alone."

2. It is inward and heart religion; 1 Pet. iii. 4. They that have no religion but what is visible to the world, have no true religion; for God is the invisible God, and walking with him must be so too; Rom. ii. 28, 29, " He is not a Jew, which is one outwardly; neither is that circumcision, which is outward in the flesh; but he is a Jew, which is one inwardly; and circumcision is that of the heart, in the spirit, and not in the letter, whose praise is not of men, but of God." It may be very hard to make any difference betwixt the life of a hypocrite and a sincere person; when the thread of hypocrisy is fine spun, it may pass the skill of the best discerner to discover it. And therefore one that walks with God, has a view beyond what he can see in others, or others can see in him. Ye must distinguish betwixt two things in religion.

(1.) The shell of it; and that is all you can see of my religion, or I of yours. This shell is religious bodily exercise, preaching, praying, works of piety, justice, mercy, and charity; 1 Tim iv. 8. These things are not very frequent in the world; but at the great day many of them will be found like deaf nuts, which being cracked and their inside discovered, are cast into the fire.

(2.) The kernel of it; and that is what none can see but God and their own consciences that have it; and that is soul-exercise, heart-work; 1 Tim. iv. 7; Acts xxiv. 16. That only is godliness, and not the other. Preaching and praying, though it were with tears and the greatest seeming seriousness, is not godliness; it is the faith, fear, love, humiliation of heart, hatred of sin, resignation to the will of God, and conformity of the heart to his mind, which is in the preaching or prayer, that is religion in God's account. It is not the works of piety, &c., themselves, but the love to God for his own sake, and love to our neighbour for his, the holiness of the principle, manner, motives, ends that is in these works, that is religion. The bodily exercise is but the vehicle, in which these sacred drops are taken.

Let no man deceive himself. No kernel grows without a shell, and none can have the power of godliness without the form of it; but there is many a shell without a kernel, and much form where there is nothing of the power.

3. It is heavenly religion; Phil. iii. 20. According to men's state and their nature, so will their actions be; for as is the tree, so will the fruit be. The heart of man, according as grace or corruption reigns in it, will tincture every thing that comes through it. Hence a natural man's very religion is carnal and earthly; Jam. iii. 15. His best things in religion smell of the earth. If a gale blow at any time on his soul, it rises low; if he sorrow for sin, it is the sorrow of the world; if he offer fire, it is strange fire. On the other hand, religion tinctures the very natural actions of one that walks with God; for this is a walking as one of another world.

Walking with God is indeed walking like one of the other world, namely, the upper world. The man conforms no more to the way of this world; Rom. xii. 2, keeps no more its course; Eph. ii. 2, but is coming through it as a pilgrim, and coming out of it; Cant. iv. 8. And,

(1.) His root in this lower world is loosed, that he may be in due time transplanted into the upper world. The believer is no more one of the "world's own;" John xv. 19. There is a certain sweetness to a man in his native soil; and so there is to natural men in the world, they are rooted in it by the greedy gripe their hearts take of it; Psalm xvii. 14. But when grace comes, that gripe is loosed, and fixes on heaven; and so that sweetness goes off, and the world turns the weary land to him; Isa. xxxii. 2. They do not find that sweet in it which others find, and which they themselves sometimes found in it. Their hearts are on the way-gate.

(2.) The other world is the main thing he has in view; 2 Cor. iv.

18. While the present world bears most bulk in the eyes of others, the world to come bears most bulk in the eyes of those that walk with God. That is their designed and desired rest, that sways them in the course of their life; their desires, hopes, and endeavours centre there. They overlook, and put on a holy regardlessness both of the good and ill of the present world, if by any means they may escape the ill of the world to come, and attain the good thereof. The purchase they design lies there.

(3.) He is making way to the other world, as a man on his journey; Cant. viii. 5; not only by the course of nature, as all others, but in heart and affections, by which the soul moves; hence the apostle says, Phil. i. 23, "I am in a strait betwixt two, having a desire to depart, and to be with Christ; which is far better." It is true, when grace is not in exercise, a believer may be for building tabernacles here, he may be very unwilling to pass over Jordan; but then he is not walking with God, but standing still. Sometimes when believers are in the dark as to their state, or for some other reasons, they may be crying, as Psalm xxxix. 13, "O spare me, that that I may recover strength, before I go hence, and be no more." Nevertheless there is never a groan they give under the body of death, never a desire they have of perfection of holiness, but there is wrapt up in it a desire to be with Christ, which is best of all.

(4.) He is conforming himself to the fashions of the other world; Psalm xlv. 10. It is his own country, being born from above; he is a pilgrim here, and therefore a man wondered at, as one of strange fashions. He sets himself to be like God in holiness, for that is the happiness of those that are above. As men serve an apprenticeship in a trade, that afterwards they may set up in it; so the life of a walker with God is an apprenticeship in holiness here, to set up in glory hereafter.

(5.) *Lastly.* He draws his great comfort from the unseen things of another world; Heb. xi. 27. The apostle will have those in the Christian race to look off to Christ, "who for the joy that was set before him, endured the cross, despising the shame, and is set down at the right hand of the throne of God;" Heb. xii. 2. When this world smiles, his chief encouragement is not from it, but from the other world. When it frowns, thence is his support; Hab. xvii. 18. This has made the saints choose rather poverty and reproach, confinement, banishment, prisons, and death, than to act against the laws of heaven; and to undergo these joyfully, while the world wondered how they could bear up under them.

4. It is lively and active religion, being a walking with the living God, wherein there is not only grace, but grace in exercise; Cant. i.

12. That is a remarkable character given to Christians; 1 Pet. ii. 5, "Ye also as lively stones, are built up a spiritual house." What! "Stones," and yet "lively? Lively," and yet "stones?" Yes. The power of godliness is a compound of these two. It makes men lively in God's matters, yet as stones for solidity; solid, yet active, such as their spirits will stir within them in these matters. There are three sorts that cannot be walkers with God,

(1.) Dead people; they must be borne to their place, for they cannot go. Unregenerate graceless people cannot walk with God. What is the reason that so few walk with God. Why, truly the most part of gospel-hearers are dead people; Eph. ii. 2; and till they be raised out of the grave of a natural state, it is not to be expected of them. There was a great cry in Egypt while one was dead in every family; but alas! there are many so in many families.

(2.) Sleeping people; they are not fit for walking; and sleeping Christians cannot walk with God; Cant. v. 2. Sometimes the saints are going pleasantly on their way in the exercise of grace; their desires, love, faith, &c., are awake and stirring. But though unwatchfulness, security creeps on; and then they must lie down, they can go no further, till the Lord waken them; Matth. xxv. 5. And this is one reason why there are so many that have the root of the matter in them, who are not walking with God at this day.

(3.) Lame and wounded people, that have got broken bones by some grievous fall into sin; Psalm li. 8. They that have a thorn of guilt in their conscience, cannot walk till it be drawn out. For the conscience is defiled, the power of grace is weakened, the soul's communion with God marred; and they cannot recover their liveliness till they make new application of the blood of Christ, and renew their repentance.

5. It is regular religion, and uniform; for he that walks with God must needs walk by a constant rule, eyeing him not in some things only, but in all; Gal. vi. 16; Psalm xvi. 8. He gives one rule of walking, extending to man's whole conversation; and so he that walks with him, walks regularly, aiming at a holy niceness, preciseness, and exactness, in conformity to that rule in all things; Eph. v. 15, [*Gr.* Noticing carefully the prints of his feet with whom he walks.] Now this imports,

(1.) A design and fixed purpose in religion, namely, a purpose of conformity to God in it; Acts xi. 23.—" and exhorted them all that with purpose of heart they would cleave unto the Lord." The words are emphatic, "that they would cleave unto the Lord," *q. d.* abide by his side; " with purpose of heart," laid down and determined beforehand. A man may do a good thing in religion, which yet will not be reckoned good indeed to him; because though he did it, he had no mind to please God in it. Religion's chance customers will never be esteemed walkers with God; Lev. xxvi. " walking contrary ;" [*Heb.* By accident, at all adventures.]

(2.) A constancy in religion, in opposition to wavering; Heb. x. 23. Hereaway and thereaway in religion is not walking with God, who " is of one mind, and who can turn him ?" Job xxiii. 13. They that walk with men, or according to their own affections and inclinations, it is no wonder to see them at one time destroying what at another time they were building up; of one way in religion to-day, and another to-morrow; for these are changeable like the moon. But walking with God, people would go even forward, and keep their way they were on; neither going off on the right hand, because others go off at the left; nor going off at the left, because others go off at the right; Prov. iv. 25—27.

(3.) An evenliness in religion, in opposition to a detestable unequalness; Matth. xxiii. 23. To run with vigour in the lesser things of religion, and move like a snail in the greatest matters of it, is not walking with God. A wide conscience in substantials, and a narrow one in circumstantials, is a conscience of a profane and godless make and mould; hence is that intimation; Hos. vi. 6, " I desired mercy, and not sacrifice; and the knowledge of God, more than burnt-offerings." A sincere conforming of ourselves to the duties required in the ten commands, summed up in love to God and our neighbour, is true holiness. Instituted ordinances are the means of holiness, which will be laid aside in heaven, when perfection in holiness is obtained. Now to be hot in these last, and cold in the other, is as detestable as to be concerned to give meat to your neighbour, while in the meantime you stab him to the heart, to take away his life.

(4.) An universalness in religion; Psalm cxix. 6. He that makes no bones of balking some steps, walks not with God. They that confine their religion to their religious actions, and extend it not to their natural and civil actions, have no religion at all. What does it avail to pretend to a tenderness of conscience in one thing, and yet in other things to swallow a camel; to a tenderness in dealing with God, while no tenderness appears in their dealings with men? Psalm cxix. 128; Matth. xxiii. 24. This is one of the causes of atheism and contempt of religion in the generation; Rom. ii. 23, 24, " Thou that makest thy boast of the law, through breaking the law dishonourest thou God ? For the name of God is blasphemed among the Gentiles, through you, as it is written."

6. It is laborious and painful religion; for it is no easy life they

have whose trade it is to walk on their feet; Heb. vi. 10. And it is no easy religion to walk with God. Religion is not a business of saying, but doing; not of doing carelessly, but carefully, painfully, and diligently. If ye would be religious indeed, ye must put to your hands to work, set down your feet to walk, run the Christian race, ply all your strength to strive to enter in at the strait gate, wrestle with all your might against principalities and powers, &c. This will be evident, if ye consider these following things, (for an easy religion is the ruin of many).

(1.) Consider the scripture-notions of walking with God, in which the life of religion lies, and you will see they imply laboriousness. It is a working and labouring; John vi. 27, "Labour not for the meat which perisheth, but for that meat which endureth unto everlasting life;" [*Gr.* work.] Here he that works not, shall not eat. It is not only a working, but a "working out;" Phil. ii. 12, a bringing the work to perfection, otherwise what is wrought will be lost; 2 John 8. Some labour is easier than other; but religion is compared to that which is the hardest labour.

[1.] It is compared to the husbandman's work, which is no easy labour, ploughing, sowing, reaping; Hos. x. 12, "Sow to yourselves in righteousness, reap in mercy; break up your fallow ground." There is no ground so hard to labour, as the hard heart is to the spiritual husbandman. No ground does so quickly and incessantly bring forth thorns and briers as the corrupt nature. And whereas the husbandman for ordinary finds his work as he leaves it, the Christian rarely finds it so.

[2.] To the soldier's labour; 2 Tim. iv. 7, "I have fought a good fight." He must watch while others sleep and take their ease, otherwise the enemy will be upon him. He must fight, he must not flee, but so fight as to overcome his spiritual enemies; Rev. iii. 21. He must pursue; Heb. xii. 14, namely, as one follows a flier, till he catch him. Heaven must be taken by storm; Matth. xi. 12. The gate is strait, there is no entering with ease; men must press into it, else they cannot come thither; Luke xvi. 16.

[3.] To the wrestler's labour; Eph. vi. 12, such as makes all the body to shake again, $\pi\alpha\lambda\eta$. They must put forth their utmost strength, as those that are agonizing, wrestling with death; Luke xiii. 24. This the Christian finds in wrestling with strong lusts and violent temptations.

[4.] To the runner's labour in a race; Heb. xii. 1. That requires patience and great eagerness; Phil. iii. 13, 14; for they must so run as to obtain the prize; 1 Cor. ix. 24.

(2.) Consider the way the Christian has to walk in towards Immanuel's land, and ye will see that religion is a laborious business. For,

[1.] It is a difficult way; though plain in itself, yet to us it is difficult to know; Cant. i. 7, 8. How much precious time do the travellers spend in disputing which is the way, that might be better improved in going forward? Nay, many spend all their days in disputing about the way, till the sun go down on them, and night overtake them, ere they have begun to set off. Many mistake the way quite and clean; Eccl. x. 15, some going in the way of bare morality, some of drowsy wishes, and some of formality, &c. And many good Christians in the way are brought to that pass, that they know not where to set down the next step; but have hard work to know the road they should take.

[2.] It is a wilderness way, and therefore very solitary; Cant. iii. 6. Canaan was a type of heaven, and to it the Israelites came through the waste howling wilderness, where they had many a weary step. An emblem of the way to heaven. There the Christian often suffers hunger and thirst, there he is bit with fiery serpents, there he is attacked by furious enemies, and there he has the Jordan of death to pass.

[3.] It is a rising, an upward way; Cant. viii. 5. The way of sin is down the hill, easy, and therefore much frequented. But the way to glory lies up the hill; and hence so many are frightened from it at first sight; and many that seem to set fair off once, are quickly out of breath, and so retire. The temple, a type of heaven, was situate on a hill, Moriah; 1 Kings x. 5. Much hard travel had some of the Jews ere they got to Jerusalem, Psalm lxxxiv. 6, 7; and when they came there, they had the hill of God to ascend into; Psalm xxiv. 3.

(3.) Consider what he has to walk through, that walks with God in the way of the life of religion. He will meet with troops of opposition, but he must break through them all. They must walk through,

[1.] Opposition from the devil; 1 Pet. v. 8, 9. No sooner does a soul set on the way of God in earnest, but the armies of hell are set in battle-array against him. The sluggard says, "There is a lion in the way," &c., but the Christian resolutely walks forward. But it is hard work when a poor Christian is engaged with a malicious and subtle devil, that has had five thousand years' experience of the black art of temptation.

[2.] Opposition from the world. The world agents the devil's cause for him, and never ceases to take the ill cause of the dragon against Michael by the end. But they that mind for heaven, must set their face against the storm, and weather all the blasts that come from that quarter. They will not want the counsel of the ungodly, but they must refuse it; Psalm i. 1; the mockeries of the wicked, but they must despise them; Psalm cxix. 51. Nay, sometimes it comes to persecution, and resisting even to blood; but they that walk with God, must go through even a sea of blood when called; Matth. xvi. 15. Daniel would not leave his prayers for thirty days, when praying was death by the law; Dan. vi. 7, 10.

[3.] Opposition from their own hearts' lusts. A man's enemies are those of his own heart; Rom vii. 24. Sometimes the false heart will be saying within the man, "Arise and let us go back to Egypt;" sometimes with Peter, "Master, spare thyself;" sometimes with Judas, "What needs all this waste?" sometimes with Pharaoh, "I will not let you go." But the Christian must, over the belly of all these, walk forward; Matth. xi. 12, "The kingdom of heaven suffereth violence, and the violent take it by force."

(4.) Consider what he has to walk over. There are some things in the Christian's way to heaven, which it may be he cannot get through, but he must go over them.

[1.] Over the belly of discouragements, Heb. x. 35. Satan plies the engine of discouragement with all his force, and often mightily prevails by it, to make the Christian halt in his Christian course. And they may long sit still, if they mind to sit till they be removed. Nay, they must even break over them and go forward, though it be hard labour to get over them, saying with David, Psalm xlii. 5, "Why art thou cast down, O my soul? and why art thou disquieted in me? hope thou in God, for I shall yet praise him for the help of his countenance."

[2.] Over the belly of stumbling-blocks laid in the way, Matth. xviii. 7. The world is ruined by offences. Some give the offence, and others take it; *i. e.* some fall in the way, and others cannot go by the stumbling-block, but break their necks over it. But he that walks with God, when he cannot get them removed out of the way, he goes over them; but will not go off his way for them, as people generally do; Job xvii. 9, "The righteous shall hold on his way, and he that hath clean hands shall be stronger and stronger."

[3.] Over the belly of their credit and reputation sometimes. Many a time a Christian must make a stepping stone of his credit, to follow his duty; as David did, when he said unto Michal, "I will yet be more vile than thus, and I will be base in mine own sight," 2 Sam. vi. 22. And it is a general rule in the practice of godliness, that they must be fools who will be wise. That is hard; but sometimes they must even make a stepping-stone of their reputation with carnal and untender professors, and lay their account with their obloquy and reproach for following their duty, as you may see Matth. xxvi. 7—10.

[4.] Over the belly of their affections and inclinations. It was Levi's commendation, " Who said unto his father and unto his mother, I have not seen him, neither did he acknowledge his brethren, nor knew his own children," Deut. xxxiii. 9. They have little sense of practical religion, that do not see they must put the knife to the throat of their own inclinations and affections many times, to follow duty laid before them by the Lord. These are not the rule of our walk; but they that walk by their own inclinations and affections, walk not with God, but walk as they that are "sensual, not having the Spirit." And this is hard work, and so much the harder when they meet altogether, as sometimes they do in the case of the godly.

(5.) *Lastly*, Consider the little strength we have to walk with; 2 Cor. iii. 5, "Not that we are sufficient of ourselves to think anything as of ourselves." We got all of us a bruise in the loins of our first parents. Even such as walk with God are healed but in part, the broken bones are but beginning to knit. Well, if the iron be blunt, he must put to the more strength; the less one has, he must make the better use of it. All these considerations shew that religion is a laborious and painful business.

Well, Sirs, a slothful easy religion is a dangerous business. Take heed to it; it will not be found walking with God. The sluggard is lost by his own sloth; he "will not plow by reason of the cold," says Solomon; "therefore shall he beg in harvest, and have nothing," Prov. xx. 4. He is the unprofitable servant; see his doom, Matth. xxv. 26—30, "Cast ye the unprofitable servant into outer darkness: there shall be weeping and gnashing of teeth." He is unprofitable to himself, for he neglects his salvation-work; unprofitable to his Master, for he neglects his generation-work. Mark the sentence; he loved darkness to sleep in, he shall have his fill of it, "outer darkness." For carnal mirth, he shall "weep." He would not work because of the cold, in hell he shall "gnash his teeth."

7. It is self-denied religion; Matth. xvi. 24, "If any man will come after me, let him deny himself." Thus our Lord Jesus walked when he was in the world; and "he that saith he abideth in him, ought himself also so to walk, even as he walked," 1 John ii. 6. Self-denial is one of the first lessons that Christ puts in the hands of his scholars, and they have need of it in practice through the whole of their conversation. In the religion of walkers with God these two things are remarkable, laboriousness and self-denial, which sweetly meet together in it, as the wings of the cherubims over the ark.

(1.) Laboriousness, working as if they were to win heaven thereby,

1 Cor. ix. 24, following holiness with all eagerness, as knowing that heaven is not given to loiterers, but labourers; and endeavouring to take the New Jerusalem as by storm. For walking with God, they look on themselves as under his eye, and therefore ply their salvation and generation-work. And the love of Christ constrains them to be serviceable to him, and to ply themselves for conformity to his image.

(2.) Self-denial.

[1.] Overlooking their work and labour, as if God had not required it, putting no confidence in it before the Lord, nor valuing themselves upon it in his sight, Phil. iii. 3; but laying the whole stress of their acceptance with God on the merits of Christ. This must needs be so; for,

(1.) He that walketh with God is acquainted with the holiness and spotless purity of himself, the exceeding breadth of his law, and the jealousy of his Holy Spirit; and therefore he cannot miss to see the imperfections of his best works in these bright glasses, and say as Psalm xix. 12, "Who can understand his errors?" and cxxx. 3, "If thou, Lord, shouldst mark iniquities: O Lord, who shall stand?"

(2.) He honours the Son, living by faith in him, Gal. ii. 20. And that is one's going out of himself for all to Jesus Christ, out of his own ill in point of practice and self-loathing, and out of his own good in point of confidence, Isa. lxiv. 6.

[2.] Overlooking their own strength for working, as mere weakness, 2 Cor. iii. 5. Self-denial makes one go out of himself for sanctification to the Spirit of Christ, as well as for justification to his blood, 1 Cor. i. 30; Isa. xlv. 24. For walking with God is a walking and leaning on him to be carried on the way, Cant. viii. 5; a staying one's self upon him, as the traveller doth upon his staff. This must needs be so; for,

(1.) Whoso tries the way of walking with God, will quickly find he is not man enough for the opposition he will meet with in the way, not able to go but as he is led, nay nor stand but as he is held up, John xv. 5. The least temptation or unmortified lust, how hard is it to one left to grapple with it in his own strength? Peter falls at the voice of a silly maid.

(2.) The scripture declares, that there is no safety in, nor good to be had from, one's working merely from his own inherent stock, Prov. xxviii. 26, "He that trusteth in his own heart is a fool." Nay there is a curse denounced on him that does so, which will cause that he will never bring his work to perfection, Jer. xvii. 5, 6, "Cursed be the man that trusteth in man, and maketh flesh his arm, and whose heart departeth from the Lord. For he shall be like the heath in the desert, and shall not see when good cometh, but shall inhabit the parched places in the wilderness." And therefore have we that watchword, Heb. iii. 12, "Take heed, brethren, lest there be in any of you an evil heart of unbelief, in departing from the living God."

8. It is humble religion, Mic. vi. 8. For howsoever any may set up before men, they must needs vail their faces when they see themselves in the presence of a holy God. Proud and conceited religion is of the wrong stamp, for it is quite unlike the Spirit of the holy Jesus; and of the saints, who, the more religious they were, were always the more humble. And the more proud and conceited professors be of their religion, be sure they are so far strangers to walking with God. Now, this humble religion will appear,

(1.) In low thoughts of ourselves, and honourable thoughts of others, in whom the image of God appears, Phil. ii. 3. Paul counts himself the chief of sinners, though the chief of New Testament saints. A high conceit of ourselves, with an undervaluing of others, is a shrewd sign of little acquaintance with walking with God. For it is impossible but the man that walks with God, must see more evil in himself, than he can see in any other, that bears any thing of the holy image of God. But he that has the foul face, but looks not into the glass, may think it more beautiful than any that he sees.

(2.) In being denied to vain glory, Phil. ii. 3. He that walks with God will not have occasion to hunt after the applause of men, unless he go off his way, and so far leave his Leader. It is a sad sign of little walking with God, to affect so much honour and respect from men, and for one to trumpet forth his own praise; a disposition smelling rank of a naughty heart, Prov. xxvii. 2, " Let another man praise thee, and not thine own mouth." John xii. 43, "They loved the praise of men more than the praise of God." It may nourish one to death, but not to life, like the chameleon, to live on air.

(3.) In refusing to stoop to nothing, whereby the honour of God, and the edification of the souls of others may be advanced; as exemplified in our Lord's humbling himself, Phil. ii. 5—8. He that walks with God will be content to make a stepping-stone of his credit, ease, &c. for these ends, counting nothing too low for him whereby he may follow the Lord. But alas! there is a cursed respect for ourselves, that so prevails with many, that they count some duties of religion below them. And their pretended credit must spread, though it should darken the heavens, and wrap up the glory of God in a cloud.

(4.) In a kindly accommodating of our spirits to humbling providences, Job i. 21. Sometimes the Lord leads his people very low, through afflictions, crosses, poverty, and wants. The humble will follow him whithersoever he goes. But the proud, nothing will satisfy them, but rising, and they will blacken the heavens with their murmurings and complaints when they are falling. But if our lot be not brought up to our spirits, let our spirits be brought down to our lot. We are on our journey out of this world, and we may come as soon, and more safely, to an happy end of it, the low way, as the high way.

(5.) *Lastly*, In an absolute resignation to the will of God, saying in everything, "Not my will, but thine be done," Luke xxii. 42. Walking with God is a following of him as the shadow does the body. It causes men put a blank in the Lord's hand, that he may fill up in it what he pleases. But so far as we come short of the great duty of absolute resignation to the will of God, we come short of walking with God.

9. It is constant religion. Walking is not a rising up and sitting down again, but a continued action, like that of a traveller going on till he come to his journey's end. Enoch walked on through the world, till he was not. It is constant in two respects.

(1.) Without interruption. It is not a religion taken by fits and starts but going on evenly; Psalm xvi. 8, "I have set the Lord always before me." Some people's religion is like an ague, wherein they have their hot fits and their cold fits. They go to and fro; they will be one day for God, and another for the devil. Whatever good mood they be found in at any time, they do not abide at it, Hos. vi. 4. And so they can never bring it to any good account; for they are always beginning, ever learning, but never come to the knowledge of the truth. These people's religion consists in two things.

[1.] Flashes, and that is all they have for heaven; flashes of affections like those mentioned, Psalm lxxviii. 34, "When he slew them, then they sought him: and they returned and inquired early after God." The spirit of holiness does not rest on them, but some light touches of his common influences they get, which do not abide. Hence with convictions sometimes, and with melted but unsanctified affections, their hearts will be as when in the time of great rain every pool is full, but quickly dry again, because it has no spring. Whereas it is otherwise with those that walk with God; John iv. 14, "The water that I shall give him, shall be in him a well of water springing up into everlasting life."

[2.] Overleaps into the holy ground; and that is all that heaven has from them; Job xxvii. 9, 10, "Will God hear his cry when trouble cometh upon him? will he delight himself in the Almighty? will he always call upon God? They do not usually feed on God's pastures, but at the table of the world and their lusts. God saw this was the temper of the Israelites, which made him say concerning them, "O that there were such an heart in them, that they would fear me, and keep all my commandments always, that it might be well with them, and with their children for ever," Deut. v. 29. They will be to-day crying Hosannah, to-morrow, Crucify him. Religion is not their element, and so they cannot abide with it, Job xxiv. 13.

(2.) Without defection and apostacy. We read of some, John vi. 66, that "went back, and walked no more with him." They cast off religion, and laid it by for good and all. These people's walking with God (if we may call it so), will be no more remembered but to their condemnation, Ezek. iii. 20. They will never see heaven; Luke ix. *ult.*, "No man having put his hand to the plough, and looking back, is fit for the kingdom of God." Lot's wife was an emblem of such; she looked back to Sodom, and God turned her to a pillar of salt, for a terror to apostates. For such he abhors, Heb. x. 38. But they that walk with God will not be,

[1.] Bribed away from him, by the allurements of the world and flesh, which is one engine of Satan whereby he makes many apostates, as Judas, Demas, &c. How many are there who have sometimes, by their addictedness to the way of God, promised great things, and so have gone on for a time flourishing? But afterwards Satan has led them aside by temptations, and always farther and farther off the way, till he has got them to cast off religion altogether.

(2.) Boasted away from him, by the severities they may meet with in following the Lord; Cant. viii. 7, "Many waters cannot quench love, neither can the floods drown it." Sometimes Satan plays the fox, by cunning wiles to draw sinners to apostacy; and sometimes the lion, to drive them to it by hardships, mockeries, hard usage, and persecutions. But religion, where it is of the right stamp, will last, whatever methods may be used to put it out.

10. *Lastly*, It is progressive religion; religion that is going forward; Prov. iv. 18, "The path of the just is as the shining light, that shineth more and more unto the perfect day." There is a mark the soul aims at when it sets off in the Lord's way; and that is perfection in holiness, and walking with God is a pressing forward to it, Phil. iii. 13, 14. Such a one is adding a cubit to his spiritual stature. When the seed of grace is sown in the heart in regenera-

tion, the man must walk with God, that so the seed may grow and shoot forth. And so in walking with God the new creature grows,

(1.) Inward, growing into Christ, Eph. iv. 15; uniting more closely with him, and cleaving more firmly to him as the head of influences, which is the spring of all other growth.

(2.) Outward, in good works, in life and conversation. Not only like Naphtali do they give goodly words, but like Joseph they are as fruitful boughs.

(3.) Upward; for their conversation is in heaven, Phil. iii. 20; in heavenly-mindedness and contempt of the world.

(4.) *Lastly*, Downward, in humility and self-loathing. Thus he that walks with God makes progress in sanctification.

There is also in it a progress in experimental knowledge of religion, 2 Pet. iii. *ult*. The traveller the farther he goes on, he knows the country the better; and he that walks with God gets Christian experience. Not only is his head more filled with raw unfelt notions, but his soul is stored with saving acquaintance with truth. The further he goes on, he becomes the more expert a traveller to the heavenly Canaan. He observes what has worsted, and what bettered his soul's case; and so will labour to eschew the one, and follow the other. And when he comes to a dark step, he can bear out the better, that it is not the first he has gone through.

Thus far of the nature of walking with God.

II. I shall next confirm this doctrine, That the life of religion lies in walking with God. In order to this consider,

1. That religion is not a matter of speculation, but of practice. Whatever light it brings into the mind, it is for moving the heart and affections. And therefore it is called the doctrine according to godliness. And the greatest mysteries of our religion are mysteries of godliness; 1 Tim. iii. 16. I think the devil may be a greater speculative divine than the best of us can pretend to be. And the apostle supposes one may understand all mysteries, and all knowledge, and yet be nothing; 1 Cor. xiii. 2. So little worth is the knowledge of religion without the practice, the word without the power.

2. All other practice of religion, without walking with God, is but bodily exercise, little worth, 1 Tim. iv. 8. The Jews wrote on their synagogue-doors, "Prayer without intention is as a body without the spirit." And where walking with God is wanting, there is the carcase of religion, but the soul of it is away. It can never be pleasing to God, because it is not agreeable to his nature, John iv. 24.

3. The great difference betwixt the sincere Christian and the hypo-

crite lies here, Phil. iii. 3, " We are the circumcision, which worship God in the spirit, and rejoice in Christ Jesus, and have no confidence in the flesh." What makes the sincere Christian differ from the hypocrite in his walk? Is it that he performs external duties? No, you cannot pitch upon one of these, but a hypocrite may perform the same? Is it that he knows and can speak of religion better? No, a hypocrite may excel a good Christian in these gifts. Is it that he has sometimes a flood of affections? No; Pharaoh, Esau, and the stony-ground hearers wanted not these. But the hypocrite never comes up to walking with God, which the sincere does, though not always.

4. Without this there is no sanctification, because without it there is no communion with God, and so no sanctifying influences. A man may pray many a prayer, hear many a sermon, and be many a year a professor of religion, and yet never be a whit the more holy unless he walk with God. All without that in this point, is but the washing of a blackmoor, labour in vain. For spiritless lifeless walking will never heal our unholy nature. Hence when the heart is away from God, the man is as "the heath in the wilderness, and shall not see when good cometh," Jer. xvii. 5, 6.

5. This is that part of religion that will remain in heaven for ever, 1 Cor. xiii. 8. Thus the happiness of heaven is held out under the notion of walking with God, Rev. iii. 4. All divine institutions tend to this. For this was the course the first Adam was set on, but broke off from; this course the second Adam held; and to be brought back to this will be man's greatest happiness. So that without controversy the soul of religion lies here.

6. *Lastly*, Our spiritual life lies in communion with God. In ourselves we are dead spiritually, being slain in Adam. Now our life is in Christ, Col. iii. 4, and we cannot partake of that life, but by communion with him, Gal. ii. 20, " I live; yet not I, but Christ liveth in me: and the life which I now live in the flesh, I live by the faith of the Son of God." It is that communion with Christ that makes men truly lively, and their religion, religion indeed, in so far as it makes men walk with God.

I shall now make some improvement of this subject, in uses of information, reproof, and exhortation.

USE I. Of information. This lets us see,

1. That the religion of those is little worth, that are utter strangers to walking with God. It is but the carcase of religion without the soul. The apostle speaks of "vain religion;" Jam. i. 26, "If any man among you seem to be religious, and bridleth not his tongue, but deceiveth his own heart, this man's religion is vain."

This is such. It is vain with respect to God's approbation, for he will never approve of it; Rom. ii. 28, 29; and vain with respect to their own salvation, it will never bring them to heaven, nor abide the trial; Matth. vii. 22.

2. True religion lies not in a form, but has a power with it causing a holy walk; 2 Tim. iii. 5. True religion is not a vain inefficacious thing, but has a commanding power with it. It is in the heart like the centurion, when it says to the man, "Go," he "must go;" and when it says, "Come, he cometh." It has a restraining power, it binds up the man from sin. Job was tempted to blaspheme, but the power of godliness restrained him. It sets the man in God's way, it keeps him on it, and causes him to go forward in it.

3. That no man has more true religion than what influences his walk. God will never measure people's religion by fair words or a shining profession, but by the course of their life and actions, in faith, love, and other moral duties. God has written his law in the Bible, has transcribed it again into the renewed heart, and they write it over again in their holy conversation.

4. There is little of the life of religion in the world, there is so little walking with God in it. There are few that have the form of godliness in comparison of those that want it; and yet but few of those who have the form, that have the power too. How few are there that eye God in all things, whose hearts go along with him as the shadow with the body, that walk with him in ordinances, in providences, in their stations and relations, and in their actions, natural, civil, and religious! O how rare is practical, inward, heavenly, &c. religion!

Use II. Of reproof. Hence we may reach a reproof to several sorts of persons, that do not walk with God.

1. Those that have never yet risen up from their sin. Walking with God is a motion of the soul from sin to sanctification; Isa. i. 16, 17. It is like the going up a stair, where the first step raiseth a man from the ground, and so he goes up by degrees till he come there where he would be. Heaven is the upper room, faith and holiness are the stairs, and the state of sin is the ground. But alas! many have not come the length of the first step yet; they are still in their sins, under the guilt of them, and under the power of them. They have not with Lazarus come out of the grave, with Matthew left the receipt of custom, nor with the palsied man risen out of their bed; and far less with Enoch do they walk with God.

(1.) Consider, we cannot say of you, "Ye are not far from the kingdom of God;" for truly ye are even as far from it as Adam led you and left you. The way to the pleasant land is long, and your day is far spent; but to this day ye have not entered on the way, nor stirred a foot from your old sins. Are ye not afraid, that your be gone day ere ye are able to undertake the journey?

(2.) If ye lie still, ye will never see heaven. As soon shall heaven and hell meet, as you shall get to heaven in that state and case. If ye sit still ye die; and therefore rise and walk, and flee from the wrath to come.

2. Those whose life is a mere wandering; Eccl. x. 15, "The labour of the foolish wearieth every one of them, because he knoweth not how to go to the city." Many spend their days thus wandering; among the creatures their souls wander, and from one they go to another; they take a miserable round in the vanities of this world, but never go beyond them to God. They wander up and down in the way of sin; sometimes they fall into one miserable course, sometimes into another, but never into the course of holiness. They walk in a round, whereof the centre is hell, and the circumference sin and vanity. All their life they go from one sin and one vanity to another, and at death, when they leave the world, they are in the same place they were in when they came in to it; *i.e.* As they were born in sin they die in it, and tumble down to hell, their miserable life being not a walking with God, but a wallowing in one puddle of sin all along.

(1.) Your thus wandering is a clear evidence that your natural blindness is not removed; Rev. iii. 17. Your plague is in your head, and so your heart cannot be right. Ye have never yet discovered the excellency of Christ the Captain of our salvation, nor the glory of the land that is afar off, and ye know not the way leading to it. Therefore your case is sad.

(2.) Remember the generation that wandered in the wilderness, died there, and never saw the land of Canaan; 1 Cor. x. 5. This will be your doom, if ye continue. Ye are walking in a mist among fearful precipices and fiery serpents; how can ye miss to fall?

3. Backsliders, that have turned their backs on God's way, John vi. 66. These, instead of walking with God, fall away from him, back to their old sins. They gave up their names to him, listed themselves under his banner, but now they have turned runaways. They came under bonds to God and his way; but they have broken his bonds, and cast away his cords from them. They once appeared on God's side, but they have got over into the devil's camp.

(1.) Your sin is greater than if ye had never set off in the Lord's way. Ye know that relapses into a disease are most dangerous, and most hopeless; and so "it had been better for you not to have known the way of righteousness, than after you have known it, to turn from the holy commandment delivered unto you," 2 Pet. ii. 21. For then men sin over the belly of more light than before, they cast a particular infamy upon the way of God, as if they would make the world to believe from their experience that Christ's yoke is intolerable.

(2.) Your condemnation will be the greater. It is a fearful word, Heb. x. 38, "If any man draw back, my soul shall have no pleasure in him." Prov. xiv. 14, "The backslider in heart shall be filled with his own ways." As the sorest fall is from the highest place, so the deepest plunge into the lake of fire is from the threshold of heaven. And when the backslider is taken in the snare of destruction, it will be a peculiar worm in his conscience for ever, that once in a day he had well nigh escaped.

4. Resisters of the Holy Ghost, whom God is using all means with to draw them to his way, but they will not come on it, Jer. ii. 25, "I have loved strangers, and after them will I go." Not only are they called by the word, but by providence. God meets some in their evil ways, like the angel with the drawn sword in his hand meeting Balaam, and yet they will not leave it. God hedges up their sinful ways with thorns, yet they break through the thorn-hedge. Their consciences tell them they are wrong, and give them many a secret blow to drive them into the way: but they follow their corruptions over the belly of their consciences.

(1.) This is dreadful and dangerous work, as being a fighting against God and against yourselves, Acts vii. 51. But though the potsherds of the earth strive among themselves, it is miserable folly to strive with their Maker. The voice of the word, providence, and conscience is the voice of God; take heed how ye entertain the same.

(2.) The issue must needs be terrible, if it be continued in, Job ix. 4. For when God judgeth, he will overcome. What can be expected of it, but that God be provoked to cease striving with you, and to lay the reins on your neck, Gen. vi. 3; Psalm lxxxi. 11, and afterwards call you to an account as wilful rejecters of salvation?

5. Enemies to the way of God, who not only do not walk in it themselves, but hinder others to walk in it, as the scribes and Pharisees, Matth. xxiii. 13. There are agents for the devil in the world, who have a malignant hatred against the power of godliness, and set themselves to quench the Spirit in others, by mocking, tempting them to sin, &c. Consider,

(1.) That is the devil's trade, and therefore a sad indication of one that is a child of the devil. Let such hear what the Spirit of the Lord says to them, Acts xiii. 10, "O full of all subtilty, and all mischief, thou child of the devil, thou enemy of all righteousness, wilt thou not cease to pervert the right ways of the Lord?" God is especially an enemy unto those that are enemies to his ways, and so set themselves to advance the devil's kingdom.

(2.) The blood of souls will be a heavy load; and such as turn others from the way of God, their blood will be upon their head. And those that set themselves that way, they need not doubt but that in such a corrupt world they will always be successful with some, Luke xvi. 27, 28.

6. Loose and licentious professors, who walk so scandalously that the world may see they do not walk with God, Jer. vii. 8—10, "Behold, ye trust in lying words, that cannot profit. Will ye steal, murder, and commit adultery, and swear falsely, and burn incense unto Baal, and walk after other gods whom ye know not; and come and stand before me in this house, which is called by my name, and say, We are delivered to do all these abominations?" There are many that profess religion, that it were telling religion they did not pretend to it. For hearken to their words, take a view of their life, there is no tenderness to be seen there. The voice is Jacob's, but their rough hands declare them to be profane Esau's. There is nothing that looks like holiness about them, but the profession of the truth; but their tongues and their lives are profane. Whoso sees them, may see their light hearts and offensive lives have nothing of the ballast of the power of godliness. Consider,

(1.) A loose and licentious life, under whatever profession it appear, argues a godless and graceless heart, Phil. iii. 18, 19. It is an easy thing for people to make a profession, which costs them not the life of a lust; to addict themselves to this or that opinion, while they do not addict themselves to the study of a holy life; to pin a new creed to an old life. But were grace in the heart, and they made partakers of the new nature, it would make them study holiness in all manner of conversation.

(2.) What will the end of that way be, think ye? See Psalm cxxv. *ult.*, "As for such as turn aside unto their crooked ways, the Lord shall lead them forth with the workers of iniquity." And if there be a hotter place in hell than another, the hypocrite that has a profession of religion, but a licentious life, shall get it, Matth. xxiv. *ult.* And their profession will serve but to make them so much the more marks for the arrows of God's vengeance.

7. Close hypocrites, whose outward conversation is blameless, but in the meantime they are strangers to the life of religion, and walking with God, "having a form of godliness, but denying the power thereof," 2 Tim. iii. 5. They go about duties, but they are strangers to communion with God; they walk blamelessly, but walk not with God; they abound in bodily exercise, but are estranged to spiritual

worship; they exercise gifts, but they have nothing of the exercise of grace. Their souls are estranged from the life of God, and are dead within them; and they are like some dead beasts, there is nothing of them profitable but the skin, *i. e.* the outward form.

(1.) Consider that religion may serve to blind your own eyes, and the eyes of the world, but not the eyes of God. The close hypocrite will be like Ahab in disguise, but the arrow hit him for all that; for there is no deceiving the eyes of the Almighty.

(2.) It will have a miserable issue. God loves to discover hypocrites, Rev. iii. 16, "Because thou art lukewarm, and neither cold nor hot, I will spue thee out of my mouth." Sometimes he withdraws his restraint that he has on them, and turns out their inside in this life before the world, as Judas, Ananias, and Sapphira. But he will not fail to do it at the great day, when every one shall be judged according to his works.

8. *Lastly,* Gracious persons, whose grace is not in exercise, who though they be spiritually alive in respect of their state, yet are not lively, but dead in their frame, Cant. v. 2. They are not walking with God as sometimes they have been, but are fallen asleep, and are going after the way of their own hearts. O Sirs, ye are off the way, and I will tell you how ye may know it. A gracious person may know that he is not walking with God,

(1.) By the decay of his love to his Guide. This was God's controversy with the church of Ephesus; Rev. ii. 4, "I have somewhat against thee, because thou hast left thy first love." And may not the Lord say to many of his people this day, as Jer. ii. 2, "I remember thee, the kindness of thy youth, the love of thine espousals, when thou wentest after me in the wilderness, in a land that was not sown?" While the soul walks with God, it keeps its eye upon Christ, and seeing him cannot but love him. But the soul loses sight of Christ; then out of sight, out of mind; and what the eye sees not, the heart rues not. A sad sign that ye are off the way.

(2.) By decay of love to the fellow-travellers; Matth. xxiv. 12, "Because iniquity shall abound, the love of many shall wax cold." There has been a day wherein the people of God have dearly loved one another, delighted to pray, converse, &c., together; and the wrong done to any one of them was, by reason of their sympathy, as done to them all. But alas! where is that now? Christian love is much decayed. What is the reason? Why, travellers as long as they are going out the road together, have a particular kindness one for another; but when they begin to stay by the way and scatter, one going to his business, and another to his, love wears off. Even so the Lord's people taking different ways, and scattering from one another, their love to each other cools.

(3.) By the decay of zeal for the honour of their Leader. If one would affront a captain on the head of his troop, all the soldiers' hearts would stir within them. But when he is left alone, there is none concerned to resent the injuries done to him. I never like that zeal, that, overlooking the substantials of religion, burns out on the lesser things. But this I will say, that were there more walking with God among us, there would be more zeal for the great things of religion; and if so, then more for the lesser things too. Were we more concerned for the kingdom of Christ within us, we would be more zealous for the kingdom of Christ without us.

(4.) By the decay of tenderness, and care to please the Lord; Col. i. 10. While David was walking with God, he was tender of the least sin, his heart smote him when he had cut off the lap of Saul's garment. But at another time he lay long under horrible guilt in the matter of Uriah, his heart being hardened. Sometimes Christians could have had no rest without the enjoyment of God in duties; but alas! at other times they are formal in performance of their duty as a task. And an evil deed will not be so heavy to them, as a rash word or vain thought would sometimes have been.

(5.) By the decay of diligence in duties, instead whereof slothfulness creeps in; Eccl. x. 18. He that walks with God will be diligent to note every step of his way; so it is an ill sign when the heart turns careless. He will be much conversant with God in the duties of religion, often found on the road to the throne, because he has much business with heaven; but when he walks not with God, he remits of his diligence, and comes far short of his former pains in his soul-matters.

(6.) By a decay of heavenly-mindedness, instead of which there creeps in carnality and earthly-mindedness. Walking with God is a heavenly life; Phil. iii. 20. And while a child of God holds at it, it tinctures all his thoughts, words, and actions with a savour of heaven; Cant. iii. 6. But when that fails, all these savour of death.

(7.) *Lastly.* By a decay of liveliness and earnestness in duties. Sometimes a child of God is like Jacob wrestling for the blessing; he is very peremptory, and will not take a naysay; Gen. xxxii. 26. Sometimes again as Ephraim, like a "silly dove, without heart," Hos. vii. 11; having neither heart nor hand to ply the throne of grace; a sad sign of not walking with God.

Now, to such I would say two things,

[1.] Horrid ingratitude is stamped on your ceasing to walk with God; Jer. ii. 31. The pleasantest and most profitable days a Christian ever has, are those wherein he walks with God; and when he gives over that, his real well days are done; Hos. ii. 7. Then his bones flourish as an herb, but otherwise they wither like the grass. Therefore may we say, " Do ye thus requite the Lord, O foolish people and unwise ?" Deut. xxxii. 6.

[2.] It is easy to go off the way, but not so to get on it again; it is easy to halt and sit down, but not to rise up again and walk. Ye had need to awake in time, lest the Lord give you a fearful wakening, either by some heavy stroke, or, which is worse, by letting you fall into some grievous guilt, as he did David.

Use *ult.* Of exhortation. Study the life of religion, in walking with God. Walk not after your lusts, nor in the way of the world, either its way of profaneness, or its way of formality; but go through the world walking with God. I offer the following motives,

Mot. 1. Ye are going fast through the world, and ere long will be at your journey's end. Time runs with a rapid course; and whether ye sleep or wake, ye will soon find yourselves pass the border of time; Job ix. 25, 26. The watch going wrong may run as fast as when she goes right; and the man that walks after his own lusts, makes as great speed to the end of his journey, as he that walks with God. And since we must walk through the world, and cannot abide here, why will we not choose the best company in our way, and walk with God ?

2. Walking with God is the only way to get safe to our journey's end; Heb. ii. 10. It was only Caleb and Joshua that got to Canaan, for they followed the Lord fully. All the world is on a journey; but there are two ways, and two companies. There is the way of holiness, and all the saints walk there, with the Lord on their head; and the end of this way is salvation. And there is the way of sin, a broad way, wherein are many roads, bare civility, morality, profaneness, and formality; all the unregenerate walk there, and the god of this world on their head, and the end is destruction. Choose ye with whom ye will walk.

3. Religion is not a matter of speculation and talking, but a matter of practice and walking with God; Psalm cxvi. 9, " I will walk before the Lord in the land of the living." Your eternal state lies at stake, which ye will never bring to a comfortable issue without this. Till ye enter on this way, ye are to begin to be religious, how long soever your standing in a profession has been. After children are born, it is long ere they begin to walk; but as soon as one is born again, and becomes a child of God, he immediately falls a walking with God.

4. There is a pleasure, a refined, undreggy pleasure, in walking with God; Prov. iii. 17, " Wisdom's ways are ways of pleasantness, and all her paths are peace." This pleasure arises from the testi-

mony of conscience, which is a feast to the soul; 2 Cor. i. 12, enough to make a sick man whole; from the intrinsic pleasantness in the way of holiness, which has a surpassing beauty in the eyes of those that are capable to discern; Psalm cxix. 97 and 165; and from the soul's communion with God which it finds in that way; Psalm iv. 6, 7.

OBJECT. But what can it do to us for a through-bearing in the world? ANSW. Very much, "having promise of the life that now is," as well as "of that which is to come;" 1 Tim. iv. 8. Those that walk with God have a promise of provision in this word; Psalm xxxvii. 3; Matth. vi. 30. It is no maybe, but as sure as the covenant can make it; Isa. xxxiii. 16, "Bread shall be given him, his water shall be sure." It is true, God's bond is not always paid as it were in money: but if not, it is always paid in money-worth, If they get not the thing itself, they get as good; 2 Cor. vi. 10,— "as having nothing, and yet possessing all things."

6. Walking with God is the best security in evil days. There are sinning and ensnaring times; who can be so safe in them as they that walk with God? even as in a dark day, those that keep closest with their guide, are likeliest to get safest through; Prov. xi. 3, "The integrity of the upright shall guide them." There are suffering times, days of common calamity; and then those that walk with God are likeliest to be brought through, as Noah; Gen. vi. 9.

7. *Lastly*. This is the way all have taken, that have walked through the world to Immanuel's land. God's children only are heirs; and they that are his children must follow him; Eph. v. 1. There is no walking with God in heaven, but for those that walk here with him in holiness. And therefore remember, "If ye live after the flesh ye shall die; but if ye through the Spirit do mortify the deeds of the body, ye shall live;" Rom. viii. 13.

I shall now shut up all with some directions, and advices for walking with God.

1. Labour to be sure ye are Christians indeed, and once fairly set on the way, by closing with Christ. Renounce the world and your lusts; and look on yourselves as men bound for another world, under the conduct of the Captain of the Lord's hosts; Cant. iv. 8.

2. Lay it down for a certain conclusion, that religion is quite another thing than mere external performances. It is a conforming of the soul to the image of Christ, and of the life and conversation to the holy law, by a participation of the virtue of his blood and Spirit. And therefore there must be constant endeavours to abide close by Jesus Christ, in the exercise of faith, love, and universal tenderness, not only in life, but in heart; Prov. iv. 23.

3. Being set on the way, labour to hold by it. Ye must learn

not to be shamed out of God's way, by the reproaches of the world. Care not for the name of singularity, and be not ashamed to be fools in the world's eyes; 1 Cor. iii. 18, 19, not to be bribed nor boasted out of God's way, by any advantage or loss in the world; Heb. xi. 24.

4. Closely ply the work of mortification; Gal. v. 24. What is your need of Christ, if it be not to save you from your sins? Matth. i. 21. Beware of making Christ the minister of sin, by going the round betwixt sinning and confessing, without suitable endeavours for mortification. Mortification is no easy business; but most necessary.

5. Beware of indulging yourselves in those things that are accounted but small sins, and abstain from all appearances of evil. No man will walk with God, to whom any sin is so small that he will make no bones of it. And those that stand not to go frankly into the borders of sin, will very readily step over.

6. When ye fall lie not still, but get up again by a new application of the Redeemer's blood, and renewing your repentance. For no man can walk so but he will stumble; but then the suitable remedies are to be improved for recovery.

7. Be frequent in self-observation and examination. Take notice how often the pulse of your affections beats. Retire into yourselves, and observe the way of your hearts and lives; Hag. i. 7. And examine yourselves often as to your state and case; 2 Cor. xiii. 5. Ask yourselves whether ye be going forward, or backward, what profit ye make of duties?

8. Be diligent observers of providence; Psalm cvii. *ult.*, towards yourselves and others.

9. Be tender of waiting on the Lord, to know sin and duty in particular cases.

10. Be diligent in all religious duties, missing none of them, and being frequent in them all. For these are the trysting places for communion with God, which they that walk with him must diligently attend.

11. Prepare for duties before ye set about them; not only public duties, but private and secret ones. For the rushing on these without consideration, is the high way to make them vain and fruitless.

12. Labour to be spiritual in all things; in religious duties seeking to exercise grace, and enjoy communion with God; and even in other things, to act as under his eye, and by influence of his command.

13. *Lastly.* Live by faith; 2 Cor. v. 7. For it is by faith that the soul is set and kept in this walk.

www.ingramcontent.com/pod-product-compliance
Lightning Source LLC
Chambersburg PA
CBHW020004050426
42450CB00005B/313